FAMILY TABLE

BY ROBERT IRVINE

The information contained herein is not intended to replace the services of trained health professionals. You are advised to consult with your healthcare professional with regard to matters relating to your health, and in particular matters that may require diagnosis or medical attention.

Second printing, 2022

ISBN: 978-0-9964223-3-8

Irvine Products, LLC
1227 N Franklin St.
Tampa, FL 33602

chefirvine.com

Creative Direction & Design: Sean Otto
Photography: Ian Spanier

Page 8 image courtesy of Cy Cyr

Page 22 image courtesy of svitlini/Shutterstock.com

Page 24 image courtesy of Ekaterina Kondratova/Shutterstock.com

Page 25 image courtesy of DronG/Shutterstock.com

Page 28 image courtesy of Lisovskaya Natalia/Shutterstock.com

Page 55 image courtesy of Atsushi Hirao/Shutterstock.com

Page 69 image courtesy of etorres/Shutterstock.com

Page 104 image courtesy of Ko Backpacko/Shutterstock.com

Page 168 image courtesy of PureSolution/Shutterstock.com

Page 175 image courtesy of Iakov Filimonov/Shutterstock.com

Images on pages 9, 10, 11, 82, 83, 86, 87, 90, 91, and 182 courtesy of the Irvine family

DEDICATION

For my parents, Pat and Walter,
who showed me how this parenting thing is done.

For Gail, who has held my hand from one end of this
Earth to the other and back again.
I couldn't do any of this without you by my side.

And for Annalise and Talia,
who will always be my center.

I love you all more than words can express.

ABOUT THIS BOOK

For those keeping track, this is my fourth book, and in the humble opinion of its author, the most essential work I've yet to produce. I feel a bit guilty saying that, like a parent picking a favorite child. Yet, when I try look at everything as objectively as I can, there is no other conclusion I can come to. This is the book that is nearest to my heart because, if successful, I believe it has the power to bring families closer together—using the place I know best, the kitchen.

My first two books—*Impossible to Easy* and *Mission: Cook!*, presented the recipes inspired by my world travels and cooking challenges on *Dinner: Impossible* in a way that could be readily put to use by the home chef. My third book, *Fit Fuel*, allowed me to share my love for cleaner fare alongside workouts and motivational advice to help readers take control of their health. This book takes aim at bigger game: your family. I want to make it easy for you to cook real, wholesome food for your family and, in the process, form a deeper bond with them.

As you turn the page from here, what you'll see on the surface is a cookbook not unlike many others. Most of the pages will be filled with recipes for family-style meals. But scattered throughout this book you will find essays that I've written on a variety of topics from physical fitness to personal development. Some of these essays are about how to better connect with your loved ones. Others are about making a positive change within yourself. All of them work toward the same end goal, which is bringing your family together.

Collectively, these essays represent what I've learned about how to be a better parent and to lead your children by setting a positive example. You'll find that a few of these essays center on blocking out the negative influence of technology. This was the topic most in need of addressing since we are, at present, drowning in technology and inundated with voices other than our own and the ones closest to us. By quieting the noise and being truly present with the people around us, simple tasks you might normally take for granted—like putting a good meal on the table—take on a deeper meaning. The meal ceases to be a time for physical nourishment and becomes something that feeds your family's soul. It's not possible to forge that kind of a connection if you've got one eye fixed on your smartphone at the dinner table.

This book isn't just about you or me. It's bigger than us. It's about what we can pass down. It's about how to set an amazing table and set a great example in the process. To that end, I want you to enjoy life with a truly fit family—physically, mentally, and emotionally. Thank you for joining me on this journey. It's an honor to have you here. It's going to be a wonderful ride, and I promise there's a lot of great food along the way.

Yours in health,

INTRODUCTION

Progress comes at a price. Each piece of technology that comes along and makes life a little easier replaces an old way of doing things. In the short term, the tradeoff always seems like a win. But these subtle changes to the way we live our lives and the pace at which we live them build up over time. At a certain point you have to take stock of what you've lost along the way.

As family units, we're at a crossroad. When we're at home—and even in the same room—a lot of us aren't really together. We're engrossed with a tiny screen in the palm of our hands,

which constantly beckons to us and insists that what is happening elsewhere is more urgent than what is right in front of us.

I refuse to believe anything is more important than those around us. The relationships we have with our loved ones are the ultimate measure of a meaningful life. Responding immediately to work e-mails doesn't add meaning. Neither does keeping up with our social media following or making sure that we read every piece of breaking news. Only love can give us meaning. And just as you need to plant seeds in a cluster in the hopes of growing a strong plant, you can't foster love

within your family—or ever be truly together—if each member retreats to their own silo.

Despite our high opinions of ourselves and what we can handle, humans don't adapt very quickly to big changes. We're still struggling to come to terms with the fast food revolution, and that came about more than a half century ago. No, fast food and frozen prepared foods didn't stop us from making home-cooked meals altogether, but they pushed us toward a place where we don't do it nearly as frequently as we used to. Smartphones and video games didn't make kids hate cooking, but they've become such a constant distraction that they have started to replace a child's basic curiosity about how things work, particularly in a kitchen. What is easy becomes routine, and routines become entrenched as a generational way of life. One recent survey showed that millennials aren't even buying cereal because it creates dishes. It's hard for me to believe, especially since dry cereal was once a technological marvel that made life easier.

It's easy to get upset about it, but getting upset doesn't accomplish anything. There's only one thing you can do: Take action and give your kids a better example. You can teach them a better way by eating more meals together at home, and even get them involved in the process. Not only is this easier than you think, it will save you time, money, and stress. In short, it will improve your whole family's quality of life.

One of my fondest memories from growing up was going outside to hit my Weider weight set while my mom watched me from the kitchen as she cooked dinner. In time I eventually came inside and started to pitch in and learn basic cooking techniques. Unsurprisingly, that wonderful memory is a combination of two things that have remained vitally important to me to this day. I have built my life and career around food and fitness.

I still love reminiscing about this because the passage of time—as it does for all great memories—has purified and magnified that moment into something perfect. As I think of it now I am struck by a powerful realization, and I must conclude the opposite of what so many people my age claim about the state of the world, parenting, and childhood today: I did not have it harder back in my day. I had it much easier.

I do not envy kids today—nor the parents of very young kids. Whatever facets of life have been made easier in the four decades since I was a kid have been outweighed by a rapidly growing number of drawbacks. Specifically, our relentless technological advancement has introduced myriad distractions that can bewilder a young mind. Much of the media kids are exposed to—particularly the unfiltered opinions and memes shared on social media—are rooted in a casual surface cruelty that mocks compassion, empathy, and fair-mindedness. Our society is as anxious and fearful now as it was during the Cold War, which is both sad and confounding.

I'm not so arrogant and pig-headed as to suggest that the ideas or recipes I share here are the cure for this insanity. But I do believe at the heart of these issues lies the fact that, as families, we've lost our center. The kitchen is, and ought to be, the heart of every home. When given the right attention, it is a place of nourishment, discovery, and togetherness. When you teach your kids how to cook with you, there is a sacredness to that. It is my contention that if you can bring your family's focus back to the kitchen, back to the dinner table, and ultimately back to each other, then you have provided them with a spiritual oasis—and the strong foundations necessary to navigate our increasingly complex world.

I do not offer my advice from some mythical elevated place or lay claim to being a perfect husband and father. Quite the opposite. If I have any authority in this area it is derived from the mistakes I've made and the lessons I've learned as a result. When my daughters Annalise and Talia were very young, I wasn't around as much as I could have been. Like many parents, I was so focused on providing, I often worked terribly long hours, missing some key moments with both of them. It fell to their mother, my first wife Karen, who home schooled them for much of their upbringing, to provide the steadiness that all kids need. Thankfully, by the time I realized that

missed moments with your kids can never come back, it wasn't too late.

Where I've always exceled: I intuitively knew how to parent by example, to trust my girls' own good judgement, and to instill respect by giving it. I learned that from my mother, Pat, and father Walter. They didn't hover over me to protect me—and it certainly wasn't because they didn't care. They loved and cared deeply for all their children—and gave them the critical space necessary to stumble, fall, learn, and rise stronger and wiser.

The essays in this book are the distillation of my knowledge of parenting and family, honed as a father, husband, brother, and son. They represent what I've learned from both triumphs and setbacks, what I believe are the most enduring truths about family, and what I believe are the most crucial tools for parents navigating a time increasingly influenced by technology.

My travel schedule is notoriously demanding: I'm typically on the road about 300 days a year. Besides my live show, filming schedule, and food and wine festivals, much of that travel time is attributed to charity work through The Robert Irvine Foundation (RobertIrvineFoundation.org) and support of the USO and other military charities. This volunteer work adds incredible purpose to my life—a powerful "why" to keep me pushing as hard as I do at a point in my career where I could very easily hit cruise control.

Unlike the early part of my career where I pushed through long hours just to establish myself, I'm in a place now where I get to give back. It's a joy to do it, and a blessing to have my wife

Gail by my side for so much of it; I wouldn't trade our past two Christmases—which we spent on tour with the USO in the Middle East—for any of the comforts we worked so hard to get.

But because I live in a far-from-typical family environment, I'm often asked how I'm able to connect with my daughters in a meaningful way. My answer is this: Every family has its challenges, and while mine might look a little different from yours, there is no challenge we can't overcome with love and attention. My girls know that whenever they need me, I'm there. In the meantime, the quality of our time together dictates the quality of our relationship—and that begins with being truly present for one another.

To my never-ending delight, we've figured out how to make this crazy life work for us. We

MY BETTER HALF It's easy to stay motivated with a force of nature like Gail by my side. We've spent the past two Christmases in the Middle East with the USO.

don't bemoan the fact that we're not always together at the same time and place. Instead we treasure what we do have. Or, as Talia so wisely said, "When we're together, we don't have to do anything to make it special. It just is special." I couldn't have said it better myself.

The strongest bonds are the ones where, no matter how much time passes between seeing someone, you're able to pick up right where you left off. I have that with my family. I want you to have that—and so much more—with yours.

CONTENTS

ROBERT'S ESSAYS

I BREAKFAST

I
BREAKFAST

BREAKFAST REALLY IS THE MOST IMPORTANT
MEAL OF THE DAY, SO TREAT IT AS SUCH.
THESE RECIPES WILL HELP YOUR
FAMILY GET THE MOST OUT OF THE DAY AHEAD.

Kale, Broccoli, & White Cheddar Frittata

191	**13G**	**13G**	**6G**
CALORIES	PROTEIN	FAT	CARBS

SERVES 8

10 large eggs

½ cup milk

Salt and pepper

1 tbsp grapeseed oil

½ Spanish white onion, small dice

2 cups sliced broccoli

2 cups baby kale

1 cup white cheddar cheese, shredded

1 Preheat oven to 425 degrees.

2 In a large bowl, add eggs and milk. Season with salt and pepper.

3 In a 10-inch cast iron skillet or non-stick pan over medium heat, add grapeseed oil and onions, and cook for approximately 4 minutes, allowing onions to get some color. Next add broccoli and kale allow to cook another 3 minutes.

4 Add egg and milk mixture. Cook on stove top for 2 minutes.

5 Place egg mixture in the oven, cook for 6 minutes and top with grated cheddar cheese.

6 Cut into wedges and serve.

Biscuits

214	**6**G	**7**G	**32**G
CALORIES	PROTEIN	FAT	CARBS

SERVES 12

2 cups all-purpose flour

2 cups 00 flour

4 tsp baking soda

¾ tsp salt

3 tbsp butter

3 tbsp shortening

2 cups buttermilk

1 In a large mixing bowl combine all-purpose flour, 00 flour, bakir soda, and salt.

2 Using a fork and your hands, incorporate butter and shortening to the flour/baking soda mixture; it should end up looking like crumbs.

3 Form a well and add buttermilk to the center. Stir in until the mixture forms a dough.

4 Dump the dough onto a floured surface and roll it over itself about five or six times, until it is about 1-inch thick.

5 Using a 2-inch round cutter, cut biscuits and place on a baking sheet.

6 Bake at 450 degrees for approximately 20 minutes, or until gold en brown.

GET THE KIDS INVOLVED   There's no law requiring perfectly round biscui (though I have to admit the photo on the opposite page looks rather sharp). Give your kids a piece of dough to cut into any shape they want. You could use kid-friendly cookie cutters, but if you don't have those, you can always let them use Play-Doh cutters.

THERE'S NO RIGHT OR WRONG WAY TO MAKE MUESLI

One of the easiest ways to get kids involved in the kitchen is to make a muesli containing oats, fresh and dried fruit, nuts, milk (cow's milk, almond, or soy are all fine), nut butter, yogurt, and honey. It makes a tasty, nutritious breakfast, but the real reason muesli is so great: There's really no way to mess it up.

I could give you a precise recipe, but that's missing the point. Here you have a chance to teach your kids about the beauty of being imprecise and "feeling" your way through the process of creating something. As you can see in the picture opposite this page, I have a lot of fun doing this with my wife Gail and my daughters Annalise and Talia. All kids, especially young ones, will have fun when they realize there are no rules to break. They'll also learn about proportion. If it looks too soupy, they can add some more oats or sliced pears and apples. If it's too dry, a little more milk and/or yogurt.

If you've ever been to my live show, you know that one of the challenges I undergo is rescuing a dish once audience members have had their way with it, dumping everything from gefilte fish to Fruity Pebbles in the same bowl. By constantly tasting, adjusting on the fly, and trusting my innate sense of proportion, I've been able to change some pretty disgusting messes into food that isn't just edible, but dishes that people actually love.

The same principles are at work when you make a muesli. When I recently did this with Gail, Annalise, and Talia, we combined just a few ingredients: oats, peanut butter, honey, almond milk, and raisins. We all tasted it along the way to make sure it was just a little sweet and that the peanut butter—which is a very powerful ingredient—hadn't taken over the entire dish. Once we had a nice consistency—not too thick, and just a tiny bit runny—we put it in the fridge. By the next morning, the oats had absorbed all the excess liquid and it had transformed into a delicious meal that was big enough for the entire family. We did it with zero planning, using only what happened to be lying around the pantry, and in less than five minutes of prep time.

Remember: Food just has to taste good. It doesn't have to be high-brow or sophisticated. I'm damn good at what I do and I have confidence that I can make any dish taste great. But your family doesn't care how long it takes to make something or what kind of techniques you had to learn to make it. I recently asked Annalise what her favorite dish of mine was from when she was growing up. You know what she said? Bacon on a Martin's roll. Yup. Something so simple that literally anyone on the planet could make it. Sometimes you've got to laugh—and be thankful that kids are so great at being honest.

CHEF'S TIP Muesli is German for "mush" or "porridge" In the States, it is typically labeled with the friendlier-sounding "parfait"—French for "perfect"—though parfaits are technically layered.

Oat Muffins

189 CALORIES

4G PROTEIN

10G FAT

22G CARBS

SERVES 12

1 ½ cups rolled oats

1 cup milk

1 cup all-purpose flour

1 tsp baking powder

1 tsp baking soda

1 tbsp cinnamon

½ tsp salt

½ cup butter, melted

½ cup brown sugar

2 eggs

1 apple, peeled, ¼ inch dice

1 Combine oats and milk in a large bowl and sit for 30 minutes.

2 Preheat oven to 400 degrees.

3 In a separate bowl whisk together flour, baking powder, baking soda, cinnamon, and salt.

4 Stir in melted butter, brown sugar, and eggs; combine to the oats and milk mixture. Next add apples.

5 Using two large spoons, divide batter among lined muffin tins.

6 Bake muffins for 20 minutes and allow to cool before serving.

Banana Smoothie

247
CALORIES

3G
PROTEIN

21G
FAT

17G
CARBS

MAKES SIX 8 OZ DRINKS

2 bananas, peeled and cut into chunks

2 cup coconut milk

2 tbsp chia seeds

8 strawberries, quartered

1 cup ice

1 In a blender add banana, coconut milk, chia seeds, and strawberries.

2 Add ice, blend until smooth, and serve.

GET THE KIDS INVOLVED No kitchen experiments are as forgiving as smoothies. You and your kids can really go wild here; let them have access to a full arsenal of fruits and veggies. First, start with the base recipe I provided above, then have the kids add their favorites, one at a time. After each ingredien is added, blend until smooth and taste. If, for instance, you find the shake is a little bit bitter after adding kale or carrots, try balancing it out with some more fruit, such as blackberries, blueberries, or peach slices.

Super Green Smoothie

135 CALORIES   **3G** PROTEIN   **7G** FAT   **28G** CARBS

SERVES 3

2 cups water

1 large cucumber, cut into 2-inch sections

3 stalks celery, chopped

2 Granny Smith apples, chopped

10 sprigs parsley

1 lemon, juiced

1-inch chunk ginger, peeled

1 cup spinach, loosely packed

1 cup kale, loosely packed

½ avocado

2 cups ice

1 Add all ingredients to blender and mix at high speed until no chunks remain.

2 Add ice and blend on high speed again until smooth.

CHEF'S TIP   One of the tricky things about making smoothies of any kind is keeping a wide variety of ingredients fresh. Oftentimes, if you don't make your smoothie within two or three days of going grocery shopping, you can wind up with a lot of waste. For that reason, frozen fruit and veggies are a great option. With newer flash-freezing methods, you don't lose any nutrients versus eating fresh, and it also eliminates the need to add ice.

BREAKFAST

Berry Orange Smoothie

201 CALORIES   **9G** PROTEIN   **1G** FAT   **42G** CARBS

SERVES 2

1 cup plain non-fat yogurt

1 banana

½ cup orange juice

10 blueberries,
   fresh or frozen

6 strawberries,
   fresh or frozen

1 Combine all ingredients in the blender and blend on high until mixture is smooth. Add ice if desired.

GET THE KIDS INVOLVED   Making any smoothie with your kids is a great way to get them interested in healthier eating. Once you've done all the necessary chopping, have them add all the ingredients to the blender and turn it on. They may not want a taste if you do every step by yourself, but once they're involved, odds are they'll give it a try.

PLAN FOR AMAZING MEALS

The first step in getting the family to sit for dinner together is making a weekly meal plan. "Planning" can give a lot of people headaches—you have enough work and worry without trying to figure out every meal for the week in advance, right? Relax. It doesn't have to be painful. When done right, meal planning can be fun and relieves a lot of stress later in the week by making life easier. And the benefits of meal planning go far beyond simplification. Here are just a few of the added bonuses.

MEAL PLANNING...
1 Keeps you healthy. When you're undecided about what to eat, your chances of eating garbage increase tenfold. Especially once you're hungry, then all bets are off. (Ever go grocery shopping when you're starving? Every bag of chips starts to look like a gourmet treat.) Unless you have the makings for a healthy meal ready to go, you stand a good chance of falling back on junk.

2 Encourages you to eat more balanced meals. How many times have you had the makings for a good dinner, but lacked a few key ingredients to make it a perfectly well-rounded one? Say you've got chicken breast and potatoes, but no fresh veggie? Planning prevents you from being stuck with incomplete meals. And try not to think of "balanced" as a purely cold, scientific term that relates solely to nutrition. Balanced meals that deliver a wide variety of nutrients are more satisfying. That means fewer cravings for junk food later.

3 Encourages you to eat a wider variety of foods. Because once you've got the week's meals all written out, repeats stick out like a sore thumb.

4 Makes cooking easier. No scratching your head and looking around to see if you've got the right ingredients. You already know you've got what you need.

5 Saves time. Making decisions takes time. As a chef and a business leader, I empower my employees to make their own decisions. I'd rather spend time later to clean up a mess than micromanage. When it comes to my personal life, I also try to eliminate as much daily decision making as I can. If you ever run into me, chances are I'm wearing a navy blue t-shirt, dark blue jeans, and a pair of black loafers. Yes, I wear pretty much the same thing every day. This is by design! Scientists have proved that your ability to make good decisions diminishes as the day wears on and you make more decisions. If you wake up in the morning and spend 15 minutes hemming and hawing over what to wear—and continue this process with other decisions throughout the day—is it any wonder you're ready to order delivery by the time dinner rolls around? You're *burnt*. And not just from a hard day's work, but from making simple things needlessly complex. When you meal-plan, you eliminate tough decisions. (Wearing the same clothes every day helps, but you don't necessarily have to go there just yet.)

6 Saves money. I'm a big believer in shopping once for the week and only going back out for the ingredients you want as fresh as possible—fresh fish being one of my sticking points for same-day purchasing. Otherwise, meal planning cuts down on trips to the grocery store. Fewer trips means fewer superfluous items find their way into your cart and send your grocery bill skyrocketing. If you're in the grocery store often, you're going to spend more money. It really is that simple. Of course, that still leaves the question of how to properly meal plan. In short, it's not difficult or time consuming. Just balance each meal with a protein, a carb, and a vegetable and go for as much variety in all three categories as possible. The recipes in this book will give you a lot of ideas on how to do this.

Getting everyone on board with the plan is also much easier than you'd think. Just involve them in the process. Ask them what they want to eat. But much in the same way you'd never ask a 2-year-old an open-ended question like, "What do you want to do today?" you want to give your spouse and kids limited multiple choice questions.

Here's an example of how to phrase it: "Okay guys, I'm cooking dinner on Sunday night. What sounds better: Dill chicken with baby steamed carrots or short ribs with cauliflower rice?" If nobody is feeling either choice, propose new options, but this is the best way to keep it on the rails.

CHEF'S TIP Meal planning doesn't mean you can never eat out or order in. I'm realistic. But to avoid chaos, write take-out into your plan, as well. If everybody tends to be very busy on Fridays, then there's your pizza night. Ordering take-out on a whim when you're overwhelmed makes it feel like a failure. Writing it into your meal plan gives you the control and keeps everything on track.

Cheese Grits

404	**7**G	**36**G	**15**G
CALORIES	PROTEIN	FAT	CARBS

SERVES 8

2 cups whole milk

1 cup water

1 tsp salt

1 cup coarse ground
cornmeal

1 cup heavy cream

1 cup butter

1 cup white
cheddar cheese

Salt and black pepper
to taste

1 Place the milk, water, and salt into a large, heavy-bottomed pot over medium heat.

2 Allow mixture to come to a boil. Gradually add the cornmeal while whisking.

3 Once all cornmeal has been incorporated, add heavy cream and cover, and lower the heat. Cook for approximately 30–40 minutes.

4 Remove from the heat and add butter, cheese, and salt and pepper. Serve.

CHEF'S TIP   Grits derive their name from their gritty texture. Once prepared they are essentially a blank canvas, making their taste as simple as their name. But they're great for any home chef—or kid—to experiment with since they can be infused with any number of savory seasonings and combined with various protein sources. Try anything. Don't let tradition hold you back.

French Toast

438
CALORIES

12G
PROTEIN

17G
FAT

56G
CARBS

SERVES 4

1 tsp ground cinnamon

¼ tsp ground nutmeg

2 tbsp sugar

4 tbsp butter

4 eggs

¼ cup milk

½ tsp vanilla extract

8 slices challah, brioche, or white bread

½ cup maple syrup, warmed

1 In a small bowl, combine cinnamon, nutmeg, and sugar, and set aside briefly.

2 In a 10-inch or 12-inch skillet, melt butter over medium heat. Whisk together cinnamon mixture, eggs, milk, and vanilla and pour into a shallow container such as a pie plate.

3 Dip bread in egg mixture, pressing lightly to help the bread absorb the liquid and coating both sides.

4 Fry slices until golden brown, then flip to cook the other side.

5 Serve with syrup and/or garnishes like fresh fruit and cinnamon sugar.

CHEF'S TIP To avoid soggy French toast, place soaked slices on a wire rack to drain excess liquid before cooking.

Scotch Eggs with Mustard Sauce

430 CALORIES   **18**G PROTEIN   **30**G FAT   **22**G CARBS

SERVES 6

8 large eggs

2 tbsp distilled white vinegar

1 lb bulk pork sausage

2 tbsp chopped parsley

2 tbsp chopped tarragon

Grapeseed or vegetable oil, for frying (about 4 cups)

1 cup all-purpose flour

Kosher salt and freshly ground pepper

¼ cup milk

1 cup panko breadcrumbs

½ cup low-fat mayonnaise

3 tbsp stone-ground mustard

1 lemon, juiced

1 Place 6 eggs in a medium saucepan and cover with cold water. Add the vinegar and bring to a boil, then remove from the heat, cover and set aside 4 minutes.

2 Fill a bowl with ice water. Using a slotted spoon, remove the eggs and immediately plunge into the ice water to stop the cooking; let sit 2 minutes. Gently peel the eggs and set aside.

3 Combine the sausage, herbs, and one of the remaining eggs in a stand mixer fitted with the paddle attachment. Mix on medium speed until combined, about 3 minutes. With moistened hands, mold the sausage mixture around the cooked eggs to completely cover.

4 Preheat the oven to 350 degrees. Heat about 3 inches of grapeseed oil in a small high-sided saucepan over medium-high heat until a deep-fry thermometer reads 325 degrees (or until a pinch of panko sizzles in the oil). Season the flour with ½ teaspoon each salt and pepper in a shallow dish. Beat the remaining egg with the milk in another shallow dish. Put the panko in a third shallow dish.

5 Roll the sausage-covered eggs in the seasoned flour, shaking off the excess. Transfer to the egg-milk mixture and turn to completely coat. Let the excess egg drip off, then roll in the panko.

6 Fry the eggs until golden brown, about 3 minutes. Remove to a baking sheet, transfer to the oven and bake until the sausage is cooked through, 10–12 minutes. Mix the mayonnaise, mustard, and lemon juice in a small bowl. Serve with the Scotch eggs.

English Muffins

284 CALORIES

7G PROTEIN

5G FAT

55G CARBS

SERVES 12

1 cup milk

2 tbsp white sugar

¼ oz active dry yeast

1 cup warm water

¼ cup shortening, melted

6 cups all-purpose flour

1 tbsp cornmeal

1 In a small saucepan heat milk. Dissolve sugar into the warm milk

2 In a separate bowl add yeast to warm water, allow stand for approximately 10 minutes.

3 In a large bowl, combine milk and yeast mixture with shortening and 3 cups flour. Using a whisk, beat mixture until smooth. Add the rest of the flour and knead.

4 Cover the dough and allow to rise, about an hour.

5 Punch the dough down. Cut into 2-inch rounds. Sprinkle dough with cornmeal. Preheat oven to 350 degrees and place dough on parchment paper. Cover and allow to rise, about 30 minutes.

6 In a sauté pan over medium heat, place muffins in the pan. Heat muffins on both sides.

7 Finish muffins by baking in oven for approximately 10 minutes.

TAKE TECHNOLOGY BREAKS

It all started with good intentions. I began using social media to foster the relationship between myself and my fans. I could show people an inside look at upcoming projects and they had a direct pipeline to me so I could answer their questions. When you say it like that it sounds so harmless. Win-win, right? Well, what began as a simple dialogue quickly spiraled into much more. Sharing a look at my work became sharing what I was doing that day in the gym or where I was eating with my wife. I began to post updates about what I was reading, watching on TV, or listening to on the radio. The more updates I posted on Twitter and Facebook, the more folks reached out with responses—and with more questions. People saw how much I was online and it created an expectation that I would always be there and I was happy to oblige. My following grew. This is the is the kind of "brand engagement" or "brand building" that a lot of companies would kill for, and I have to admit that in the beginning, it felt good.

But then I was forced to question it. If I was really doing all this posting for the sake of my business, then why was it still going on when I was hanging out with Gail, Annalise, and Talia? Why did I feel a constant nagging compulsion to pull the phone out of my pocket at the dinner table and tell people what I was eating? Or to write to someone 1,000 miles away and answer their question about how to properly pan sear a salmon filet? Why couldn't that wait?

Were these strangers more important to me than my family? Certainly not. Did I lack discipline? That's never been an issue for me in the past. So then what was it? It turns out that science can help explain. Our brains are designed to crave new information. Mother Nature knew that the more we learned, the better off we'd be. Therefore, every new piece of information you receive creates a small dopamine release in your brain. Dopamine is the same chemical that is released during any pleasurable experience; this includes healthy behaviors like eating good food or having sex or exercising—and it also includes pleasurable but hazardous experiences like smoking a cigarette, doing hard drugs, gambling a big pile of money, or eating something with a lot of sugar. In short, not all dopamine releases are created equal.

In the case of information gathering, the kind of dopamine release that you might get from learning something useful by reading a book or attending a lecture is not equal to the kind you get from an endless barrage of internet news stories, viral videos, or a notification that you just got some new followers. The former serves an evolutionary purpose and should be repeated. The latter, if left unchecked, can overload dopamine receptors and force you back to the information trough (your phone or computer) for longer and longer periods of time to get the same high you got when you started. Simply stated, internet and social media addiction are real and can be highly problematic.

The phenomenon has been linked to anxiety, depression, and stress. In April of 2017, depression became the No. 1 disability worldwide. While there is still a lot more research to do on this topic, we can safely say that the rise in depression and the explosion of social media and internet usage are linked in some fashion, if not inextricably.

So what can you and your family do about it? I suggest that you cut phone use drastically; start with a dinner-table ban on phones, then expand it to a full-day technology fast on Sundays, then try to expand it to the whole weekend.

LOSE THE PHONES

I once went to an early movie premiere where the studio collected everyone's cell phones before they entered the theater. Fears of piracy and spoilers getting out made this a must. As you're attempting to bring your family closer together, I want you to borrow from this example. Set a shoe box by your front door. When everyone gets home from school and work, the phones go in the box and stay there until after dinner. Announce your intentions by saying something like this:

"We all have busy lives, so that means dinnertime is our best chance to connect. But it won't work if we try to do it while checking Facebook every five minutes. On Monday when everyone gets home, you're going to see a shoe box by the door. I want you to turn your cell phone off and put it in the box. I'm going to put the box away until after dinner. Sound good?"

There will be some objections. Most of them can be answered with, "I'm not asking for much; just that you make a small sacrifice for the family. Give it a chance and I promise you're actually going to like not being constantly distracted."

AFTER DINNER ACTIVE

After dinner, ask everyone to go outside. A light, brisk activity after eating wards off lethargy, helps you digest, and prevents the family from retreating to their techno-cocoons. Make after-dinner physical activity a regular thing and you'll reap not just long-term physical benefits, but you'll also further strengthen your bonds with one another.

Here are a few of my favorite after-dinner activities for the whole family:

A brisk walk: No one can say they don't know how to do it.

Bike ride: The swift-moving scenery stimulates the mind.

HORSE: A low-intensity basketball game for everyone that doesn't require any actual basketball skills.

Hide-and-seek: If you've got very young ones, they'll go nuts for it. If you've got older kids, it'll get a bit more competitive!

Frisbee: I recently played Ultimate Frisbee with Gail and the girls for the first time and was kicking myself for not introducing it to them sooner. It's a blast!

Light activity isn't intense enough to burn fat or build muscle, but it accomplishes something far more important in the minds of your kids: It normalizes physical activity as routine. Most people avoid physical activity after a meal. Instead, they try to save anything physical for an ideal time of day when they're not too tired, hungry, or full. This is a mistake. Our bodies are designed to move all the time, not just during some hypothetically perfect window. Show your family that they can go grab positive endorphins whenever they want. They're just a brisk walk away.

Sunday Morning Oatmeal

171	**3G**	**2G**	**37G**
CALORIES	PROTEIN	FAT	CARBS

SERVES 4

1 ½ cups water

1 ½ cups whole oats

½ tsp kosher salt

½ cup dried cherries

½ cup golden raisins

1 tbsp brown sugar

1 tbsp milk

1 banana, sliced

1 Heat water in a saucepan. Bring to simmer. Add the oatmeal and salt. Bring to a boil.

2 Lower heat and simmer for approximately 8 minutes, stirring.

3 Remove from heat and stir in dried cherries, raisins, brown sugar and milk. Cover and allow to sit for 3 minutes.

4 Serve and top with banana.

CHEF'S TIP Oatmeal is another great blank slate for you and your kids to experiment with. In addition to the recipe above, here are three other flavor combinations that really work great: almond and cherry; apple and cinnamon; and my favorite, ricotta and fig.

Blueberry Oatcakes

382	**9**G	**14**G	**58**G
CALORIES	PROTEIN	FAT	CARBS

SERVES 4

2 cups rolled oats

2 large Granny Smith apples

2 large ripe bananas

2 large eggs

Cinnamon

1 tbsp vanilla extract

1 cup whole milk

3 tbsp butter

1 cup blueberries

1 Grind oats into oat flour, using a coffee grinder or food processor (You can also buy pre-packaged oat flour). Core the apples, leaving the skin on, and cut into large chunks.

2 Combine oat flour, apple chunks, bananas, eggs, 5–10 dashes cinnamon (depending on preference), vanilla, and milk in a blender Slowly mix until fully blended. Do not overmix. The batter shoul be thick, not runny.

3 Melt butter over hot griddle. Ladle the mixture onto the griddle in $1/3$-cup scoops. Push blueberries into the pancakes; flip once the edges are firm, cooking about 3–4 minutes per side.

4 Serve hot and top with real maple syrup if desired.

CHEF'S TIP   You'll need to have just a little more patience than you typically would with a regular wheat-and-sugar pancake batter; these cook just a little bit slower, but are well worth the wait. You may not even want the syrup (and its extra calories) since the sweetness from the apples and bananas really shines through in the finished product.

Orange-Scented Yogurt with Strawberry Compote

243	**15G**	**1G**	**45G**
CALORIES	PROTEIN	FAT	CARBS

SERVES 3

3 cups non-fat plain
  Greek yogurt

2 oranges, zested
  and juiced

10 strawberries quartered

¼ cup agave nectar

1 lemon, juiced

½ cup hemp seeds

½ cup chia seeds

1 In a large mixing bowl add yogurt, orange zest, and juice and mix.

2 In a medium 2-quart sauce pot add quartered strawberries, agave nectar, and lemon juice.

3 Place 1 cup of yogurt in a bowl top with hemp seeds, chia seeds, and strawberry compote.

DON'T WAIT FOR THE RIGHT MOMENT

"Do not wait; the time will never be 'just right.' Start where you stand and work with whatever tools you have at your command, and better tools will be found as you go along."
— *Napoleon Hill, Think and Grow Rich*

Napoleon Hill was writing more directly about entrepreneurship and business, but the above maxim applies to all forms of goal-setting. The desire to have all of our "ducks in a row" before we begin a big project or start a new career is a natural one, but I agree with Hill that it is a faulty one.

I should know. I'm more than a little predisposed to perfectionism, but I've learned that trying to grasp for control of every variable is a fool's errand. It's impossible to control for everything. At a certain point I had to ask myself where I would be today if I had insisted on perfection from the outset. The answer: Not very far.

Think about it. At the start of your career, when you were first trying to find your footing, things were probably a little haphazard, weren't they? You tripped and fell, learned from your mistakes, and moved on. That was certainly true for me in my life—as a chef, dad, husband, and businessman. From the mistakes I made in all areas, I found a better way.

Perfectionism kills dreams. I see it especially in the fitness industry, where the pursuit of the perfect diet, training routine, and ultimately, body gives rise to a strain of perfectionism that stops action on the spot. The industry is filled with people who invariably dream big, but they be-come too rigid to break from their routines and go get what it is they really want.

I was recently out at the Arnold Classic and I met tons of eager young men and women and shook their hands and heard their stories. A lot of them told me about businesses and websites they wanted to start, supplements they wanted to formulate, programs and books they wanted to write, and dozens of other ideas. They all wanted to make an impact on the world. But so many of these grand ideas were in the gestational stage of their lives. They were big, beautiful dreams, but most of these folks hadn't acted on them yet.

When I asked them why they hadn't started, they all gave me some variation of the same excuses—that they were waiting for the right moment/enough money/the right business partner/more time/etc.

To them, and to you, I say to heed the words of Napoleon Hill and realize that there is no such thing as the right moment. Progress and success are messy things that don't happen in a straight line. You take a step forward and then you have to take a step back. You reach the top of the hill and then you're knocked down. There is no escaping this, so there should be no shame in it. Every failure holds a lesson if you look for it; you can apply those lessons to your career, to your fitness journey, to your own personal development.

Let go of perfectionism and pursue what you really want. We are all just a heartbeat away from eternity. So live today like you cannot fail. Because if you never quit, you'll never fail.

II

SIDES & STARTERS

RECIPES FOR A SNACK TO TEASE THE TASTE BUDS
OR THE PERFECT FLAVOR
COMBINATION TO COMPLEMENT YOUR MEAL.

Broccoli-Quinoa Salad
& Sriracha-Buttermilk Dressing

301	**4G**	**24G**	**20G**
CALORIES	PROTEIN	FAT	CARBS

SERVES 6

BUTTERMILK DRESSING

1 cup buttermilk

2 tbsp sriracha hot sauce

3 tbsp grapeseed oil

1 tbsp lemon juice

1 tsp rice vinegar

Pinch of freshly ground
  black pepper

1 tsp fine sea salt

SALAD

1 medium red onion, sliced

2 small heads of broccoli,
  cut into bite-size florets

1 cup quinoa

Kosher salt to taste

½ cup parsley, chopped

¼ cup cilantro, chopped

¼ cup pistachios, chopped

½ cup golden raisins

4 oz Parmesan cheese,
  grated

BUTTERMILK DRESSING

1 Whisk buttermilk, sriracha, oil, lemon juice, rice vinegar, pepper, and 1 tsp sea salt in a medium bowl. Taste and season with more salt if needed.

SALAD

1 Stir together onion and 2 tbsp buttermilk dressing in a small bowl and set aside.

2 Cook broccoli in a large pot of boiling salted water until crisp-tender, about 1 minute. Using a slotted spoon, transfer broccoli to a bowl of ice water; let cool. Drain and place on a kitchen towel–lined baking sheet.

3 Return water in pot to a boil and cook quinoa until slightly al dente, about 12 minutes. Drain. Toss quinoa and 2 tbsp buttermilk dressing in a large bowl to coat. Season with salt. Let cool.

4 Add dressed onion, broccoli, parsley, cilantro, pistachios, raisins, and 2 tbsp buttermilk dressing to quinoa. Toss to combine. Layer cooked quinoa on bottom of serving dish. Top with broccoli salad. Finish with grated Parmesan.

Optional: Serve with chicken, steak, or fresh grilled seafood.

GET THE KIDS INVOLVED With any dressing and sauce recipes in this book, once you've measured out the ingredients, let your kids mix them together. Teach them to do it in a firm, but controlled manner so nothing spills out of the bowl as they do so. They'll learn an appreciation for the chemistry of food and, in this particular recipe, how disparate ingredients like buttermilk and sriracha combine to change color and create something entirely new and complementary. Have them take a taste of the buttermilk, a (tiny) taste of the sriracha, and then have them taste the new creation. They'll stop thinking of food in a static state, but as a living canvas where they can apply their creativity.

Shrimp Fried Rice

311	14G	12G	38G
CALORIES	PROTEIN	FAT	CARBS

SERVES 4

2 tbsp grapeseed oil

20 16/20 or jumbo peeled deveined shrimp

Kosher salt

8 scallions, whites chopped, greens thinly sliced

2 garlic cloves, chopped

1 tbsp finely chopped and peeled ginger

3 cups cold cooked white rice

2 large eggs, beaten to blend

4 large eggs

½ cup frozen edamame, thawed

½ cup frozen peas, thawed

3 tbsp reduced-sodium soy sauce

2 tbsp unseasoned rice vinegar

1 tsp toasted sesame oil

1 Heat 1 tbsp oil in a large nonstick skillet over medium-high heat. Season shrimp with salt and cook, turning once, until just opaqu in the center, about 3 minutes. Transfer to a plate.

2 Heat remaining 1 tbsp vegetable oil in same skillet; add scallion whites, garlic, and ginger. Cook, stirring, until fragrant, about 1 minute. Add rice and 2 beaten eggs, stirring constantly. Cook un til rice is crisp and eggs are cooked through, about 2 minutes.

3 Pushing rice to one side of skillet—or in a separate skillet—fry 4 eggs sunny side up until the whites are cooked through, about 3–4 minutes. Set aside.

4 Add edamame, peas, soy sauce, vinegar, sesame oil, and cooked shrimp to rice. Cook, tossing constantly, until shrimp and vegeta bles are heated through, about 1 minute. Top with fried eggs and scallion greens.

CHEF'S TIP   Cook the rice, either in a pot or rice cooker, according to package instructions the night before you make this meal. This eliminates a time-consuming step and will get the family seated much quicker.

GET THE KIDS INVOLVED   This is a great way to entice kids to eat seafood. Stand side by side with them as the shrimp cooks. Showing your kids that it onl takes three minutes per side will teach them how easy it is to make, and hopeful foster an appreciation for seafood, which most Americans don't eat enough of.

WHY YOU SHOULD TREAT YOUR KIDS LIKE ADULTS

It's almost impossible not to do it. Whenever you see a baby, your voice raises an octave, you simplify your grammar, and you talk "like a baby," repeating your words over and over. It's perfectly natural and serves an evolutionary function too: According to one study, kids who are exposed to this kind of speech have a vocabulary twice the size of kids who don't hear it by the time they're 2.

The problem I see with a lot of parents is that the use of simplified speech toward their kids continues well past the toddler years, right up to teenage years. It's not "baby talk" per se, but it doesn't sound like normal conversation between two adults. I see it all the time: Friends with kids aged anywhere between 6 and 16 talk to those kids a little louder, clearer, and simpler. This is just a modified kind of baby talk, and it doesn't take long for a kid to start interpreting the slow, booming way you ask them, "Did you clean your room?" or "Will there be any parents at this party?" as a lack of respect for their intelligence. By trying to bring yourself down to their level, you're assuming that they wouldn't be able to mentally stay with you if you just treated them as a peer.

To make matters stickier, you may not be wrong. Your kids very well might be able to better understand you when you simplify and amplify your speech. But in my experience, the long-term upside of speaking to them as peers is much bigger than the short-term benefit of—let's call it what it is—talking down to them. This goes for not just the tone of your voice, but also the words you use and the concepts you convey.

From the time my two daughters Annalise and Talia were 5 years old, I spoke to them like adults. I gave them space. I let them pursue what they were interested in. In the kitchen, I let them handle sharp knives. There were always boundaries. There was always supervision, but I did my absolute best to make sure they could learn and experience things for themselves without their constantly sensing the boundaries around them.

I understand the impulse of all the helicopter parents out there, but making mistakes and occasionally getting hurt are two of the most essential components of learning. Of course I always wanted my girls to be safe. But I'd rather have them get some bumps and bruises along the way if it meant having them grow up strong enough to handle their troubles on their own.

Try this: Assume your kids are tougher, smarter, more resilient, and more resourceful than you are—because they probably are.

> Try this: Assume your kids are tougher, smarter, more resilient, and more resourceful than you are—because they probably are.

Then show them the world the way you'd show a friend visiting from another country. Take them to art-house movies (you should screen them first), high-end restaurants, art museums, concerts, and poetry readings. Don't assume that, because of their age, they won't be interested. They might very well tell you they hate it and that they'd rather stay home and watch the new Pixar movie. But give them the option. Expose them to ev-erything within your own good judgment. If they're anything like my girls, you'll eventu-ally be able to send them out into the world well-cultured, sociable, and confident. They won't have to deal with the all-too-common post-high school culture shock that makes them want to crawl back into their shells. Best of all: They'll be smart enough and capable enough to contribute something of real value to this wonderful world of ours.

Roasted Carrots
with Cilantro Pesto

95	**2**G	**9**G	**4**G
CALORIES	PROTEIN	FAT	CARBS

SERVES 6

12 baby carrots, peeled and
  cut in half

2 ½ tbsp grapeseed oil

3 cloves garlic

4 oz Marcona almonds

1 bunch cilantro

1 lemon, zested and juiced

1 Preheat oven to 400 degrees.

2 In a large mixing bowl, season carrots with salt, pepper, and 1 tbsp oil. Spread carrots on a baking sheet and bake for 10 minutes.

3 In a food processor, add garlic, Marcona almonds, and 1 tbsp of oil. Puree. Add cilantro and continue to puree. Add lemon zest and juice. Finish with last ½ tbsp of oil.

4 Pull carrots from oven and finish with cilantro pesto.

Lemon-Poppy Beets

97	7G	4G	10G
CALORIES	**PROTEIN**	**FAT**	**CARBS**

SERVES 4

1 tbsp plain Greek yogurt

½ lemon, zested and juiced

Salt and pepper

3 red beets

1 tbsp grapeseed oil

1 tsp poppy seeds

1 orange, zested and cut
   into slices

1 tsp pistachios, chopped

1 Preheat oven to 375 degrees.

2 In a large mixing bowl, add yogurt, lemon zest, and juice. Season with salt and pepper.

3 Place beets in a foil packet, sprinkle with salt and pepper, and ru with oil. Fold packe closed and place on a baking sheet. Bake for 60 minutes.

4 Peel beets and cut into 1-inch cubes.

5 Toss beets with yogurt and orange slices, and finish with chopped pistachios.

CHEF'S TIP If you like the sweet and tart flavor combination on these beets, try the same recipe but replace the beets with carrots.

New England Clam Chowder

584	**35**G	**38**G	**20**G
CALORIES	PROTEIN	FAT	CARBS

SERVES 12

2 tbsp grapeseed oil

2 leeks, cleaned and
   cut in 1-inch pieces

4 shallots, small dice

10 cloves garlic, minced

2 white onions,
   small dice

2 celery roots, small dice

2 lbs bacon

3 cups white wine

1 qt clam juice

1 qt chopped clams

1 qt water

5 bay leaves

1 qt heavy cream

½ tsp cayenne pepper

1 In a large sauce pot over medium heat, add grapeseed oil, leeks, shallots, garlic, and onions. Allow to sweat for about 8 minutes.

2 Add celery root and bacon, and allow to sweat for another 5 minutes, being sure not to get any color on the vegetables.

3 Add wine and bring to a boil. Allow alcohol to cook off, approximately 5 minutes.

4 Add clam juice, clams, water, bay leaves, and cream and bring mixture to a simmer. Allow to simmer for 45 minutes.

5 Finish by seasoning with salt and cayenne pepper.

THE JOYS OF LIVING
WITHOUT DISTRACTION

If you took my advice back on Page 34, you've now banned smartphones at the dinner table. No one died. No one's work or social lives suffered. No one had painful withdrawals. It turns out that this family of yours actually likes being around each other and talking to each other. It turns out the distractions we constantly seek were merely habitual, not a desperate escape from the mundane.

You made it this far, so I want to encourage you to take the next big step and try this advanced technique: A full-day, or full-weekend, technology detox.

A full-day tech detox might look like this: You cook breakfast while the kids play outside, you eat, then head to the park after breakfast to play some games (try Poleish or KanJam!) and eat a packed lunch. Then you kick back, relax, and maybe take

a siesta, or read a magazine, newspaper, or book. Then you head home for dinner, after which you gather everyone around for a board game or jigsaw puzzle.

It might sound like a little much on paper, but once you get going with it, you're not going to want to break the streak. You'll think to yourself, "I haven't checked email since Friday when I left work, and it feels amazing!" If you're anything like me, you'll get competitive with yourself and try to see how far you can push it.

When it comes to the afternoon siesta/downtime/reading time, I can guarantee you that someone in your family is going to raise a serious objection to keeping the phones away. "But I read on my phone," they'll say. "I'd rather check in on my friends," they'll say. Your job in this situation is not to stick to your guns or be the tyrant. Your job is to, as politely and lovingly as possible, try to get them to see your point of view and to choose it for themselves. Show them a better way and they'll usually choose a better way.

Tomato Salad

269
CALORIES

49G
PROTEIN

1G
FAT

9G
CARBS

SERVES 12

3 lbs ripe tomatoes

1 tbsp grapeseed oil

1 tbsp balsamic vinegar

4 lb low-fat buffalo
mozzarella

1 bunch basil, ripped

1 Cut tomatoes in quarters.

2 Place tomatoes in a mixing bowl and dress with grapeseed oil, balsamic vinegar, and sea salt and mix.

3 Cut or rip mozzarella into small pieces and incorporate to salad.

4 Finish with torn basil on top.

CHEF'S TIP   You can use regular fresh mozzarella made from cow's milk, but buffalo mozzarella offers a richer, creamier consistency and flavor. The low-fat variety, as used in this recipe, is also high in protein. You can opt for the whole milk variety, but be aware that it will pack a lot more fat.

Roasted Sweet Potatoes

221	**5**G	**10**G	**29**G
CALORIES	PROTEIN	FAT	CARBS

SERVES 8

2 tsp granulated sugar

8 peeled sweet potatoes, medium dice

1 bunch sage

1 shallot, finely chopped

2 tbsp lemon juice

½ cup walnuts, cut in half and toasted

3 oz gorgonzola blue cheese

1 Pre-heat an oven to 400 degrees.

2 In a small pot, add sugar and ½ cup of hot water together, and allow sugar to dissolve.

3 Toss sweet potatoes in the sugar and water solution with sage.

4 Remove from water and gently pat dry. Bake sweet potatoes in over for approximately 7–10 minutes. Add shallots to roasting pan. Return to oven for an additional 7–10 minutes.

5 Pull from oven and toss in lemon juice. Top with walnuts and gorgonzola cheese.

Mashed Potatoes

363	**7**G	**21**G	**62**G
CALORIES	PROTEIN	FAT	CARBS

SERVES 6

4 lbs Russet potatoes, peeled and quartered

4 tbsp salt

2 cups heavy cream

3 tbsp butter

White pepper, to taste

2 tbsp chives, chopped

1 Place potatoes in a large pot and cover with cold water.

2 Add 4 tbsp salt. Bring potatoes to a boil and allow to simmer for about 20 minutes or until potatoes are tender.

3 Strain potatoes, place cream and butter in a small sauce pot.

4 Put potatoes through a ricer or a food mill.

5 Using a wooden spoon, add warmed butter and cream mixture. Season with salt and white pepper, and chopped chives.

GET THE KIDS INVOLVED   Let your kids do the mashing. I remember watching the potatoes ooze between the metal grates of the potato masher as a kid and being absolutely hypnotized by it. And it's more fun than playing with Play-Doh because you don't get in trouble for eating it when you're done!

Sweet & Sour Collard Greens

145	**8**G	**8**G	**13**G
CALORIES	PROTEIN	FAT	CARBS

SERVES 6

1 tbsp grapeseed oil

3 slices bacon, cut into 2-inch cubes

1 large onion, medium dice

3 cloves garlic

1 lb fresh collard greens, cut into 2-inch pieces

3 cups chicken broth

3 tbsp sugar

2 tbsp apple cider vinegar

Pepper, to taste

1 In a large pot over medium heat, add grapeseed oil and bacon, and allow to render. Remove bacon from the pan.

2 Add onion and garlic, and allow to sweat about 5 minutes.

3 Add collard greens and cook for approximately 5 more minutes, making sure to stir.

4 Add chicken broth and cook over medium heat for 45 minutes.

5 Finish with sugar, vinegar, and pepper to taste.

STAY CONSISTENT, EXCUSES BE DAMNED

There are a lot of reasons so many busy families wind up eating out more often than not. I call it the illusion of all or nothing—the idea that you need to get everything right over the course of a day, week, or month or else there's no point in doing anything right at all. This is how a fridge fills up with leftover pizza and Chinese takeout. This is why, instead of getting up to go to the gym before work, you keep telling yourself that you'll do it after the holidays, or once you get back from vacation, or after so-and-so's going-away drinks next week. If you give yourself the opportunity, there's always a reason to procrastinate. There's always another mile marker to wait for. "I'll get right back on track after this…"

It's natural to think this way. No one really wants to consider going to the gym after work if they slipped up and had a doughnut in the break room that afternoon. Those two things are incompatible in our minds. They don't go together and so if we indulge in the former we want to skip on the latter.

Life, however, is full of ups and downs. There is no such thing as a perfect day, week, month, or year. You will lose willpower from time to time. You will slip up. But as sure as I'm sitting here writing this, I'm telling you that the only way to deal with a misstep is to get right back on track—immediately. Don't push it till tomorrow or Monday or any other time. Get right back on it now. Do what you can right now. At this very moment, pick something that you can do to improve your health—and do it today. Not tomorrow or next week. Your future self will be a collection of all the tiny choices you make along the way, so make as many good choices as you can whenever you can. Those little choices to do something good—even when you're having an overall bad day—can add up quickly.

A good analogy for this approach is this book, which is my fourth. None of the books I've written were written from start to finish without interruptions or setbacks or the need to rewrite large sections or without having to throw out recipes that were terrific but ultimately impractical for the reader. The piles of discarded copy and recipes and ideas are far bigger than the finished product you see. The process itself is full of fits and starts, good days where I get a lot done and bad days when I only get a little done. But the point is, I'm always getting something done. If I have a big project to do, I don't let a day go by where I don't make some progress, where I don't do at least one good thing to further the process.

My overall health and eating habits are governed by the same concept. I mean to get to the gym four or five times a week for a nice long training session, but with my travel schedule that's not always possible. Sometimes I only have 20 minutes, but I'll take that 20 minutes and make something out of it. I won't just sit around and regret not having more time.

Remember: It's never too late in the day to do something good for yourself. Prep a healthy breakfast for the morning. Do 20 pushups. Tell your family how much you love them. Then sit down and visualize how much better tomorrow is going to be.

Maple & Bacon Brussels Sprouts

260	7G	12G	44G
CALORIES	PROTEIN	FAT	CARBS

SERVES 8

18 Brussels sprouts

2 tbsp maple syrup

1 tbsp apple cider vinegar

3 tbsp grapeseed oil

3 slices bacon, rendered and cut into 1-inch pieces

1 Prepare the Roasted Sweet Potatoes recipe on Pg. 60.

2 Cut Brussels sprouts in half lengthwise from top to bottom.

3 In a separate bowl, add maple syrup and apple cider vinegar, and whisk in 2 tbsp grapeseed oil.

4 In a sauté pan, add 1 tbsp of grapeseed oil over medium to high heat. Place Brussels sprouts in the pan and cook for approximately 4 minutes on each side.

5 In a separate bowl add Brussels sprouts, bacon, and roasted sweet potatoes. Dress with maple vinaigrette and serve.

Beet & Miso Soup

493 CALORIES	**10**G PROTEIN	**32**G FAT	**45**G CARBS

SERVES 8

½ lb butter

2 Spanish white onions, medium dice

5 red beets, peeled and quarted

3 large Yukon Gold potatoes, peeled and quartered

2 cloves garlic, minced

2 tbsp miso paste

3 qt vegetable stock

2 cups heavy cream

Salt and pepper

4 tbsp Greek yogurt

1 In a medium sauce pot over medium-high heat, add butter and onions, and allow to sweat for about 3 minutes.

2 Add beets, potatoes, and garlic, and allow to sweat for another 2 minutes. Add miso and vegetable stock. Allow to come to a boil.

3 Add cream and bring back to a boil.

4 Season with salt and pepper, and puree in a blender.

5 Serve and garnish each bowl with 1 tbsp yogurt.

CHEF'S TIP   Beets are one of my favorite root veggies. Along with a distinct flavor, they add fiber and a good amount of vegetable protein to your diet. This recipe transforms them into a rich, sweet soup that everyone will enjoy. Try serving it with grilled cheese for an upscale twist on the classic tomato soup pairing. Parents, you can also feel free to pair this with a nice glass of sake.

Grilled Mexican Street Corn

195 CALORIES

9G PROTEIN

8G FAT

27G CARBS

SERVES 2

2 ears of corn

1 lime, zested

2 tbsp queso blanco

1 oz bacon lardons, chopped

1 tbsp cilantro

LIME AIOLI

2 egg yolks

1 lime, juiced and zested

2 cloves garlic

2 tsp Dijon mustard

Salt and pepper

1 tsp grapeseed oil

1 Peel both ears of corn, and soak in cold salted water.

2 Place corn on a hot grill, approximately 3 minutes on each side.

3 To make lime aioli, put all ingredients in a blender and pulse until thickened.

4 Finish corn with lime aioli (1 tbsp on each ear), lime zest, bacon lardons, queso blanco, and cilantro.

Irish Soda Bread

338	8G	2G	75G
CALORIES	**PROTEIN**	**FAT**	**CARBS**

SERVES 8

2 ¼ cups all-purpose flour

½ cup cake flour

1 tsp baking soda

1 tsp baking powder

½ cup light brown sugar

1 tsp salt

1 cup raisins

1 cup quick-cooking oats

1 cup currants

1 tsp caraway seeds

1 cup buttermilk

12 oz Guinness stout

1 tbsp vanilla extract

1 Preheat oven to 425 degrees.

2 Prep a cake pan, smearing it with butter and flour.

3 In a large mixing bowl add all–purpose flour, cake flour, baking soda, baking powder, sugar, salt, raisins, quick-cooking oats, currants, and caraway seeds.

4 In a separate bowl add buttermilk, beer, and vanilla extract.

5 Form a well in the middle of the dry ingredient mixture, add the wet ingredients to the flour mixture.

6 Incorporate with your hands, it will look more like a cake batter than a bread dough

7 Add the batter to the butter and floured pan bake for 40 minutes or until a toothpick comes out clean.

8 Cool bread on baking rack allow to completely before serving.

CHEF'S TIP   When not serving this straight out of the oven, cut into slices and warm them in a toaster oven. Or, for a decadent twist, melt some butter in a hot pan and fry the slices on each side; you'll get warm, crispy edges and flavor that makes this a very satisfying dessert. For something completely different, use this as the bread in my French toast recipe on page 30. It's *amazing*!

SUGGESTION & EXAMPLE– A PARENT'S MOST POWERFUL TOOLS

I was a scrawny little kid when a teacher first suggested that I play rugby. You might have looked at me and pegged me for a soccer player, not someone who could take the physical punishment of the rugby pitch. So why would a well-meaning adult plant such an idea in my head? Because he wasn't concerned with my lack of muscle mass. He saw my broad frame and realized what I could become. In other words, he set me on a new path based on my *potential*, not based on where I was at that moment. Of course I did play, subsequently fell in love with weight training, and joined the military. The rest, as they say, is history. It was a seminal moment in my life and I owe it to the fact that someone showed a bit of faith in me and nudged me outside my comfort zone.

Your influential power as a parent is even greater. It might not feel like it when your kids actively rebel against your authority and seem hell-bent on doing the very opposite of what it is you tell them to do, but the power is there, subtly working its magic every day whether you realize it or not.

I've learned that our power as parents resides in two primary tools: suggestion and example. You use the first tool simply by suggesting to your child that they might try something. It's best employed like this. Say you have a child younger than 8 years old. You hear them singing along to a pop song and you say something like, "That's amazing! I bet you could be a famous singer someday." It plants a seed of confidence and helps them overcome fear of judgment. You can encourage your child to nurture his or her talent without asking them to do a thing. You just made a suggestion. If the suggestion is appealing to them, they'll pursue it. If it's not, they won't.

With an older child, say in his or her teens, it works pretty much the same way, but needs to be a bit subtler. In this instance you hear them singing along to a pop song and you say, "That's really good. Did you ever think of taking lessons? I bet with a little training you could make a career of that someday." In this instance you can have a bit more of a dialogue and, if your child is receptive, offer to pay for lessons if they're interested. In either case, suggestion is a far more effective tool than asking them to do something outright or worse yet, making demands. Suggestion puts them in the driver's seat and can work for encouraging an unlimited number of positive pursuits.

I used this technique with my daughters countless times and it worked wonders. It worked so well I decided to use it in business. I've built a small but powerful company over the past decade or so. We produce everything from television shows to healthy foods to kitchen products to health, fitness, and motivational advice published via my digital magazine (RobertIrvineMagazine.com). Across all departments I have a team of over 30 people working for me and I hand selected each one of them. If you know anything about me, you know I want the best of the best. And that certainly holds true when I choose who works for me. From my executive chefs to my business and marketing heads, every single one of my employees are highly sought-after in their respective fields. And—not to toot my own horn too much—but their earning potential and career opportunities exponentially increased after joining my team. Why? Not because of the raw celebrity power of working with me. No, it increased because I entrusted each of them to do things they had never done before.

I asked them to show me growth and innovation and creativity on a scale that none of them had ever actually executed in the past, because the typical workplace doesn't ask for that. But I saw in each of them the potential for more. The vote of confidence from me—the *suggestion* that they were capable of greater feats than they had ever attempted—helped set each of them on a path to building something truly special. I place a tremendous amount of value on each of my team members and I'm incredibly grateful for their contributions. Like any good boss, I clearly communicate my expectations and I express my gratitude when those expectations are met. But unlike most other bosses, I show faith in my employees to do that which has not yet been done—and I get more by using this kind of healthy suggestion than sheer demands could ever produce.

The second, and in my opinion, even more powerful tool at your disposal is

example. Kids won't always ask for your advice or approval, but they will, subconsciously or otherwise, model their behavior after yours. This can hold true whether you provide a positive example or not. What's more, kids don't have a static opinion of who you are and what you stand for. They don't look at your weight or disposition or occupation and form a concrete image of exactly who you must be. Their minds are pliable and more open than most adults, so if you stay committed to learning and evolving and constantly expanding your horizons, they will take notice. They will begin to learn that graduation into adulthood does not mean the end of personal development.

If, on the other hand, they witness you spending a lot of time in your comfort zone, then that will become an appealing place to them. Subconsciously, their own comfort zones will start feel like destinations on a map, instead of the waypoints they ought to be.

Ideally, you would use both of these tools in conjunction with one another. When my teacher set me on a path to play rugby and everything that followed, he did so using both tools. First, he made an appealing suggestion that showed faith in my potential. Second, he had the bona fides to back up what he was talking about. He wasn't a man who had ever settled into some kind of comfort zone. He was a dynamic, passionate teacher who got the most out of the kids he worked with because he demanded nothing but the best from himself. Kids pick up on that kind of an example. I picked up on that. Set a similar example worthy of emulation and your kids will pick up on it, too.

Mason Jar Salad

291	8g	10g	25g
CALORIES	**PROTEIN**	**FAT**	**CARBS**

SERVES 4

2 oz avocado oil

1 oz red wine vinegar

1 tsp Dijon mustard

$^1/_4$ tsp black pepper

$^1/_8$ tsp kosher salt

$^1/_2$ cup chopped red onion

$^1/_2$ cup sliced cucumber

1 cup chickpeas, cooked

$^1/_2$ cup sliced bell pepper

$^1/_2$ cup sliced hearts of palm

$^1/_2$ cup halved cherry tomatoes

$^2/_3$ cup cooked freekeh

4 cups spinach

1 oz feta cheese, crumbled

1 Combine oil, vinegar, mustard, pepper, and salt into a mason jar, shake to make dressing then divide into four mason jars.

2 Divide onion, cucumber, chickpeas, bell pepper, hearts of palm, tomatoes, and freekeh into all four jars, top with the spinach and feta.

3 Shake jar to distribute dressing before serving. Eat straight from the jar, or empty contents into a bowl.

Corn Salsa

216	**6**G	**10**G	**35**G
CALORIES	PROTEIN	FAT	CARBS

SERVES 4

15 oz can of corn, rinsed

4 oz poblano pepper, diced

16 oz roma tomato, diced

8 oz red onion, diced

1 bunch cilantro

1 avocado, diced

2 limes, juiced

Kosher salt and pepper,
   to taste

1 In a large mixing bowl, fold all ingredients together.

1 Serve with tortilla chips.

CHEF'S TIP   When it's in season, fresh corn on the cob is preferred over the canned variety. Husk and boil three ears for about 7 minutes, let them cool (or run them under cold water), then slice the kernels from the cob and add to the other ingredients.

Grilled Peach & Arugula Salad

174	6G	192G	11G
CALORIES	**PROTEIN**	**FAT**	**CARBS**

SERVES 6

4 ripe peaches

3 tbsp grapeseed oil

1 tbsp white wine vinegar

1 shallot, minced

1 tsp honey

2 cups baby arugula

3 slices bacon, cooked and cut into 1-inch cubes

1 tbsp gorgonzola blue cheese, crumbled

1 Cut peach into quarters, coat with grapeseed oil, and season with salt and pepper.

2 Place the peaches on hot grill. Cook for approximately 4 minutes on each side.

3 In a separate bowl, add white wine vinegar, shallots, and honey and slowly add grapeseed oil.

4 In a separate bowl, add baby arugula, bacon, and grilled peaches and dress with the white wine vinaigrette you just made.

5 Finish salad with crumbled gorgonzola.

EMBRACE YOUR INNER CHILD

Every person on this planet was born with creative energy that is urgently trying to express itself. For children, this comes naturally. They don't carry the adult burden of being self-aware, so they have no reservations about singing, or dancing, or painting, or doing whatever pops into their heads that feels right. Adult frustration with children often stems from the apparent randomness of it all. Parents know their kids will act out, get messy, or get into trouble, but the unpredictability of it can be irritating. This is because children are perfectly tuned into their nature and respond to it. That's why they might want to play in the mud when we've dressed them up for a party or they might decide to scream and shout when they're supposed to observe a moment of silence. They're not choosing to be agitators or drive us up the wall—although it can certainly seem that way. They're just being true to their nature—staying fully attuned to their innate creativity—unencumbered by the norms we try to impose.

We would all do well to remember what it was like to play as a child. To write or sing or pick up a musical instrument and just play—without any concern of whether anyone would think it was good or original. We fear criticism and embarrassment and so we block ourselves off from our creative energy. Choosing not to express this isn't just sad, it's life-threatening. Creative energy needs to express itself. If you don't turn it outward, it will turn inward, and inevitably create a host of fears and neuroses that will come to define you.

The good news is that you don't need to have any predilection to the creative arts to express this energy. There is no job or household chore to which creative energy cannot be applied. This is especially true for cooking. You do not need to make sushi like Iron Chef Masaharu Morimoto to express artistry in the kitchen. Creativity can be a part of every step of the process, from prep to cooking to plating. Not surprisingly, then, the truth of this statement becomes quite clear when you involve a child in the process.

Kneading dough might seem like yeoman's work, but a child will see a thing of wonder to be marveled at and played with. Children will also find the musical rhythm in whisking a bowl of eggs where we see something that just needs to get done quickly. When the crust on a chicken pot pie turns golden brown and steam rises from the slits, you see that dinner is ready. A child, meanwhile, sees it for what it really is: magic. As well they should! You just combined separate ingredients to create something entirely new!

You can introduce your children to the world of wonder and creative exploration that exists right within your kitchen. But first you need to remember what it was like to be a child and begin to believe again.

MEET
ROBERT
NYCWFF.ORG
OCT 16-19

food network NYCWFF
PRESENTED BY FOOD&WINE
NEW YORK CITY WINE & FOOD FESTIVAL
EAT. DRINK. END HUNGER.

Robert Irvine's
e t!

85

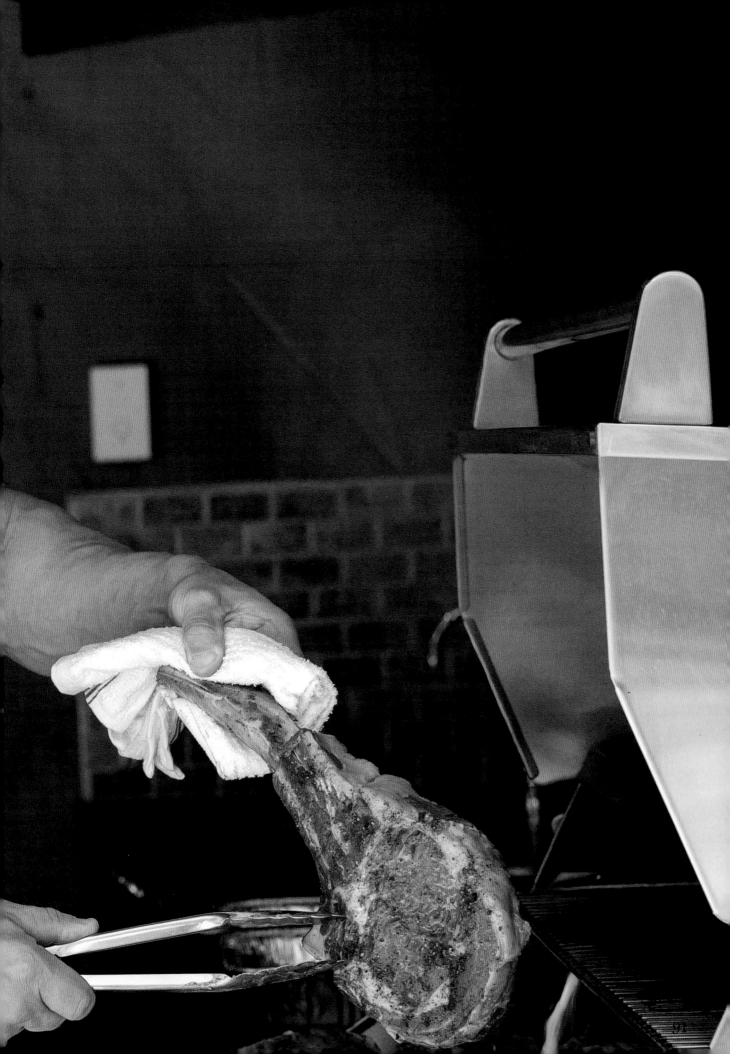

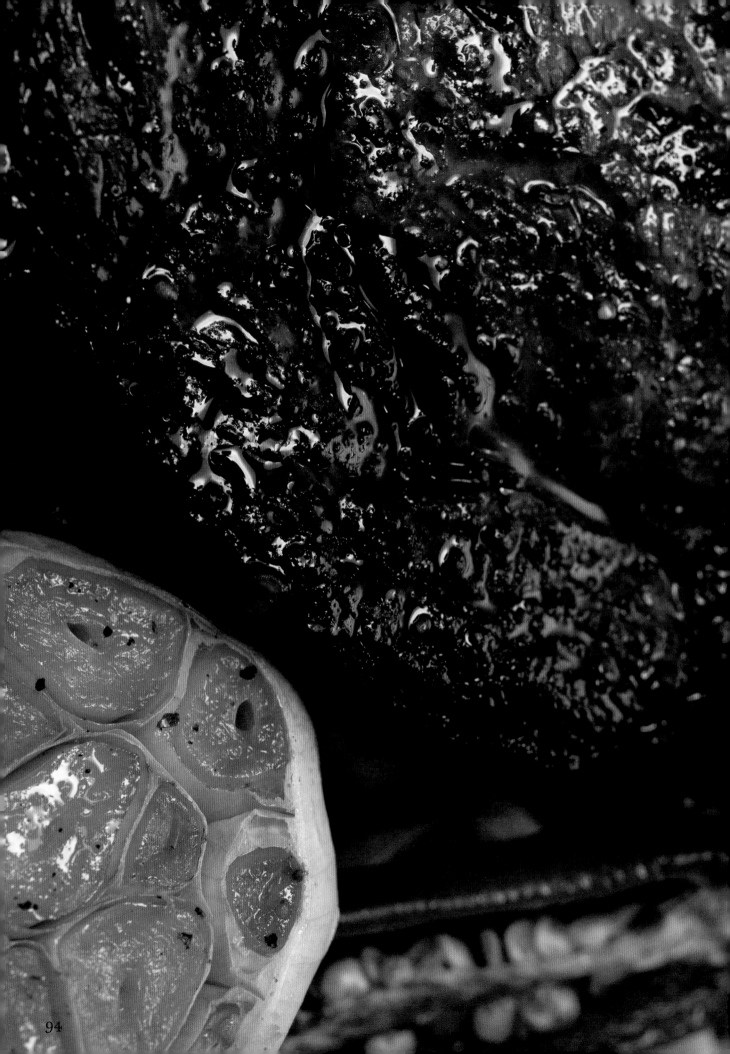

III

MAIN DISHES

DON'T JUST CALL THE FAMILY TO
THE DINNER TABLE. COOK SOMETHING
UP THAT WILL MAKE THEM RUN THERE.

Pan-Seared Cod
with Curry Rice

463	**43**G	**13**G	**42**G
CALORIES	PROTEIN	FAT	CARBS

SERVES 6

FOR THE FISH

2 lbs cod, without skin

½ cup Wondra flour

2 tbsp grapeseed oil

3 tbsp white wine

1 ½ tbsp heavy cream

2 tbsp lemon juice

1 tbsp orange juice

1 tbsp capers

2 tbsp chopped parsley

4 tbsp butter, cut
 into cubes

FOR THE RICE

1 cup white basmati rice

2 cups water

1 tsp salt

2 ½ cups chickpeas

1 tbsp curry powder

1 oz cilantro

1 tbsp sunflower seeds

COD

1 Season each piece of fish with a liberal coating of salt and pepper

2 Dredge in flour (be sure to pat off excess flour).

3 Add oil to sauté pan over medium-high heat, then add fish to pan. Sear fish for approximately 3 minutes on each side. Fish should still be slightly under cooked.

4 Pull fish out of pan, discard oil, and return the pan to heat.

5 Add wine, heavy cream, lemon juice, orange juice, capers, and parsley, and reduce by half.

6 With a whisk slowly add cubed butter, creating an emulsion. Once you have added all the butter, add seared fish back to pan an finish for approximately 5 minutes.

RICE

1 Preheat oven to 325 degrees.

2 In a quart sauce pot, add rice and water, bring water to boil, and add 1 tsp of salt. Cook in oven for 12 minutes. Pull rice from oven and cover, allowing to steam for 6 minutes.

3 Pull cover from rice, with a fork stir rice gently, adding chickpeas, and being careful not to beat up rice.

4 Add curry powder, cilantro and chicken thigh to rice. Stir with sunflower seeds and more cilantro if desired. Serve with fish.

Flank Steak with Jicama Salsa

255	**31**G	**13**G	**1**G
CALORIES	PROTEIN	FAT	CARBS

WITH $\frac{1}{4}$ PORTION OF SALSA, ADD:

128	**0**G	**14**G	**2**G
CALORIES	PROTEIN	FAT	CARBS

SERVES 4

FOR THE SALSA
¼ cup tomatillos, diced
¼ cup tomatoes, diced
¼ cup jicama, diced
¼ cup olive oil
Cilantro, to taste
2 tbsp lemon juice
Salt and pepper, to taste

FOR THE MARINADE
1 tbsp jalapeno, chopped
1 tbsp garlic, minced
1 tbsp olive oil
1 tbsp lemon juice
2 8 oz flank steaks

1 For the salsa, combine chopped tomatillos, tomatoes, jicama, oil, cilantro, and lemon juice. Add a pinch of salt and pepper.

2 Cover in plastic wrap and place the salsa in the fridge.

3 For the marinade, combine chopped jalapeno, garlic, oil, and lemon juice. Blend.

4 Allow flank steak to marinate overnight.

5 Grill or sauté for about 4 minutes on each side, or until internal temperature reaches 135 degrees.

6 Cut steak at an angle.

CHEF'S TIP If you find your cutting board sliding as you slice, place a wet paper towel underneath it to eliminate shifting.

The tuber jicama is a great base for a steak-paired salsa. Its crisp texture and fresh taste make it the perfect base for the tomato and tomatillo blend. Whip th salsa up the night before to give the flavors time to meld.

Classic Flank Steak

159 CALORIES **32**G PROTEIN **30**G FAT **4**G CARBS

SERVES 2

1 8 oz flank steak
2 tbsp balsamic vinegar
1 tsp Dijon mustard
2 garlic cloves, minced
3 tbsp grapeseed oil
3 sprigs basil, chopped

1 In a mixing bowl add balsamic vinegar, Dijon mustard, and garlic.

2 Slowly incorporate grapeseed oil. Add basil.

3 Marinate steak for at least 3 hours, though it can sit for up to 24 hours.

4 Place steak on a hot grill, cook for approximately 5–8 minutes or until steak reaches desired temperature.

5 Serve as medium rare (recommended) or an internal temperature of 125 degrees.

CHEF'S TIP   Flank steak is a lean and relatively cheaper cut of meat, and un-like a strip or ribeye, doesn't have a lot of fat to keep it juicy and tender through-out the cooking process. That's where a longer marinating time comes in handy; you'll also want to keep the cooking temperature on the medium-rare side. If yo like your meat well-done, opt for a more naturally tender cut, such as skirt steak

SHUT OFF THE TV AND GET TO BED

When actor Henry Cavill was training to get in shape to play Superman in the comic book blockbuster *Man of Steel*, his trainer demanded a lot. But besides the many hours of grueling workouts and the strict diet that you'd expect, Cavill's trainer had a third requirement: Get 10 hours of sleep every single night, a little more than the recommended 7-9. The reasoning behind this was twofold: 1) muscle doesn't grow in the gym while you lift, but while you are at rest, and 2) there was no chance Cavill would have the energy to give his all to the intense workouts ahead if he wasn't

getting a lot of sleep every single night. For the record, unless you're trying to portray a superhero onscreen, I don't think you need 10 hours, but everyone needs 7-9, and very few of us actually get it. And I can already hear the protests now... *But Robert! I function just fine on 5 or 6 hours of sleep! Been doing it for years, thanks!*

In response, I will first say this: Beware of any urgent impulse you have to decry a concept as something that's not possible for you. We all have our blind spots; by definition, those blind spots reside in the places we refuse to look.

I understand, too, why you want to skip

this advice. You want to skip it for the same reasons I do! You work too damn hard and for too many hours to just shut your brain off and get to bed early. You earned some time to watch TV or surf the internet, dammit! Maybe even have a cocktail, too. But this logic is faulty for a few reasons. By not getting to bed early and giving yourself a shot at an optimal amount of sleep, you're making everything in your life more difficult: from being productive at work to being an effective parent to having the energy to get to the gym. And that's to say nothing of how much your mood and physical health could improve by committing to more sleep.

Studies have proven that getting enough sleep can help you lose fat, improve your mood and memory, reduce inflammation, lower your stress levels, decrease your risk for depression, and increase your lifespan. In short, when you get more sleep you're going to feel more alert, focused, and creative.

Getting there is simple, but not easy. It's simple because all you have to do is get yourself into a dark room with no screens at an early hour. There's nothing to buy and no advanced techniques to learn—and yet it's difficult because most people just aren't used to it. They're used to having the TV on or scrolling through their phone—or both. Breaking this cycle is like ripping off a bandage—one that's stuck on with superglue. It's going to hurt, but it has to be done. Once you do it, you're free to rediscover the glorious analog world of printed books and magazines and a soft light by your nightstand. These work better to in-duce sleep than any prescription drug.

As for those of you who like to read but prefer to do it on a phone or tablet: It's not that simple. Reading on paper doesn't bombard your pupils with sleep-disrupting blue light the way a computer, phone, or TV does. Reading off of paper soothes the eyes and makes it easy to fall asleep. Reading from a lighted device makes it much harder to do so. (I'll allow that some e-readers, designed to mimic the experience of reading on paper, are better than a regular phone or tablet, but there's no substitute for the real thing. Besides, if your e-reader can get on the internet, it's not a good thing to take to bed with you.) As for your devices? Charge them in another room or turn them off entirely.

Do the hard work of pushing yourself through this for a week. After that it will get easier and you're going to start looking forward to it. You're going to feel more energized in the morning, happier and more productive throughout the day, and you'll be a more attentive and effective parent. It's going to a be huge, positive difference in your life—one everyone around you is going to notice, especially your kids.

Obesity is directly linked to lack of sleep for several reasons: When you don't get enough sleep you don't want to exercise; when you're up late you tend to eat more; and lack of sleep disrupts the hormones that control appetite. It's a domino effect with compounding results that worsen with time. But by setting the right example and getting to bed early, you're giving your kids a powerful tool that will help them live healthy for the rest of their lives.

> By setting the right example... you're giving your kids a powerful tool that will help them live healthy for the rest of their lives.

Cumin & Coriander Skirt Steak

STEAK WITH MARINADE

367
CALORIES

49G
PROTEIN

19G
FAT

1G
CARBS

SERVES 4

FOR THE STEAK
24 oz skirt steak
2 tbsp cumin
2 tbsp coriander

FOR THE BLACK BEAN SALSA
¼ cup red onion, diced
¼ cup roasted red pepper, diced
2 tbsp cup cilantro
1 cup black beans
2 tbsp vinegar
2 tbsp olive oil
Salt and pepper

1 Mix cumin and coriander thoroughly.

2 Rub into flank steak. Grill or pan sear for about 4 minutes on each side, or until internal temperature reaches 135 degrees.

3 While the steak cooks, combine red onion, roasted red pepper, cilantro, black beans, vinegar, olive oil, and salt and pepper.

4 Serve steak garnished with salsa.

Grilled Shrimp & Pineapple Salad

483 CALORIES	**36**G PROTEIN	**25**G FAT	**34**G CARBS

SERVES 4

FOR THE SALAD

1 lb (16-20) fresh shrimp, peeled and deveined

¼ pineapple, diced

1 head Bibb lettuce

1 head romaine lettuce

12 cherry tomatoes, halved

1 bulb fennel, sliced thin

½ red onion, sliced thin

1 ear corn, grilled and cut from the cob

1 avocado, diced

FOR THE DRESSING

½ cup orange juice

2 cloves garlic, minced

2 egg yolks

1 thumb ginger, minced

1 oz grapeseed oil

1 oz chili oil

1 Season shrimp with salt and pepper, and place on a hot grill. Cook for 2–4 minutes on each side.

2 For the dressing, add orange juice, garlic, egg yolks, and ginger into a food proccessor.

3 Slowly add grapeseed oil and chili oil while pulsing the processor.

4 Season with salt and pepper.

5 In a separate bowl, add pineapple, lettuce, tomatoes, fennel, red onion, and grilled shrimp.

6 Add dressing. Toss and serve and top with corn and avocado.

Fresh Crab & Corn Spaghetti

369 CALORIES	**20**G PROTEIN	**15**G FAT	**41**G CARBS

SERVES 6

4 whole ears of corn

2 slices bacon

1 tbsp butter

1 qt vegetable stock

2 lbs spaghetti

3 tbsp shredded
Parmesan cheese

2 tbsp heavy cream

1 tbsp black pepper

6 oz crab meat

1 Begin by shucking the corn and removing the kernels with a knife by standing the ears up vertically and running your blade between the kernels and the cob.

2 Place the bacon in a pan over medium high heat with 1 tbsp of butter. Render the fat from the meat and heat until butter begins to brown. Add corn and allow to cook for approximately 3 minute Next add vegetable stock and bring to a boil.

3 In a separate pot of boiling water, cook spaghetti. This should take approximately 10 minutes.

4 Add spaghetti to corn broth and finish with Parmesan cheese, heavy cream, black pepper, and crab meat.

GET THE KIDS INVOLVED   Kids make good sous chefs, so put them to work! Shucking corn might feel like grunt work to you, but it'll make a kid feel useful because it's an important part of the process.

COMMIT TO CONTINUOUS GROWTH

"Love dies only when growth stops."
— Pearl S. Buck

"Strength and growth come only through continuous effort and struggle."
— Napoleon Hill

"Growth is never by mere chance; it is the result of forces working together."
— James Cash Penney

So much of what holds us back from pursuing a new goal is that it's hard to see ourselves at the finish line. We can state our goal to lose 50 pounds and try to imagine what that feels like, but sometimes, with a very big goal, the imagining rings hollow. We can see it in our mind's eye, yet not really believe what we see. This is a product of the goal seeming too far away because we haven't yet taken any concrete steps to get there. For example, you could use your imagination to picture what it would feel like to score the winning touchdown in the Super Bowl, but if you've not a pro football player, your mind has no trouble sorting this into the "fantasy" column. Meanwhile, you can easily imagine what it will feel like to do a routine task like picking your kids up from school or eating a good meal. These are things you have experience with and so your brain accepts them as likely outcomes.

To go back to the analogy of losing 50 pounds, until you've lost at least 5–10 pounds, it's hard to begin imagining what losing 50 will feel like without your brain dismissing it as fantasy. This isn't a problem, per se, it's a natural defense mechanism of the brain, which always seeks to draw clear lines between fantasy and reality. In essence, your brain is saying, "Until you take some real steps toward this, let's not even go there. I'll let you imagine it, but it won't feel real."

In this scenario, your mission is clear: 1) Take some concrete steps and lose the first few pounds and 2) Continue to imagine the best possible outcome. Through action and continued positive expectation, you'll get there. And the more steps you take—i.e., the more your actions mirror your beliefs—the more the process will feel easy and natural, with the positive outcome a foregone conclusion.

This is growth, or personal development, distilled. Do you remember what it felt like to be in third or fourth grade? Do you remember what it felt like to look up to the kids in high school? Did you naturally imagine what it might be like to be in high school yourself? If you're anything like me, it was very difficult to imagine. When you're 9 or 10 years old, high school seems so impossibly far away that imagining what it might be like feels like fantasy. Only by growing does it start to feel like a close eventuality. Then, by the time you're 12 or 13 and on the doorstep of high school, it's quite easy to imagine.

For too many of us, the end of physical growth and pre-set milestones like grad-

uation mark the end of our growth and development as individuals. It doesn't have to be this way—and it absolutely shouldn't. You can carry that universal experience of growth with you for the rest of your life if you choose to. You just have to make a commitment to keep on growing—not stop at 18 the way so many of us do. What is next for you? Is it weight loss? A better life for your family? A career change? Whatever it is, you can get there if you make the decision to continuously imagine the best possible outcome and take action toward your goals.

New York Strip Steak with Black Bean Salsa

881	**93**G	**48**G	**12**G
CALORIES	PROTEIN	FAT	CARBS

SERVES 2

FOR THE STEAK

2 8 oz hanger steaks

1 tbsp lime juice

1 clove garlic

1 bunch cilantro, chopped

3 tbsp grapeseed oil

BLACK BEAN SALSA

1 cup black beans

½ cup roasted red peppers diced

½ cup red onion, diced

1 tbsp paprika

1 tbsp cumin

1 tsp salt and pepper

½ cup parsley, chopped

1 tbsp olive oil

1 tbsp lime juice

1 tbsp rice wine vinegar

1 In a mixing bowl add lime juice, garlic, cilantro, and grapeseed oil

2 Marinate hanger steaks and refrigerate for at least 3 hours and up to 12 hours.

3 Pan sear hanger steak for approximately 5 minutes per side, or until internal temperature of 125 degrees.

4 In a large bowl add black beans, roasted red peppers, red onion, paprika, cumin, salt, pepper, chopped parsley, and olive oil.

5 Finish with lime juice and vinegar.

GET THE KIDS INVOLVED   Measure out the marinade ingredients, then let your kids combine, add the meat to the dish, cover, and refrigerate. There's almost no part of the process they could really screw up, so you might as well let them do the entire thing while you watch. When the family sits down to ea they'll feel proud of what they made, as they should!

Roast Chicken
with Sweet Potatoes & Oranges

616 CALORIES	**36**G PROTEIN	**38**G FAT	**34**G CARBS

SERVES 8

8 skin-on, bone-in
 chicken thighs

Kosher salt to taste

8 garlic cloves, minced

3 tbsp lemon juice

5 tbsp grapeseed oil

1 large or 2 medium sweet
 potatoes, scrubbed

3 large sprigs rosemary

2 oranges, thinly sliced

2 oranges cut in half for
 squeezing

15 oz chickpeas, rinsed

½ cup green olives, pitted

4 oz feta cheese, crumbled

1 Preheat oven to 450 degrees. Place chicken in a large bowl and season with salt. Add garlic, 2 tbsp lemon juice, and 2 tbsp oil, and toss to combine.

2 Let sit at room temperature at least 30 minutes or cover and chil up to 12 hours. Remove chicken from marinade, draining off any excess; discard marinade. Set chicken aside.

3 Prick sweet potato all over with a fork and roast on a small foil-lined baking sheet until tender, about 1 hour. Let sit until co enough to handle.

4 Once potato comes out of the oven, start cooking the chicken. Heat 1 tbsp oil in a large skillet—preferably cast iron—over medium-high heat. Cook chicken, skin side down, until skin is very brown (it should get very dark; as long as you don't smell it outright burning it will be all the better with some char), about minutes.

5 Transfer to oven and roast, keeping skin side down, until cooked through, 18–22 minutes. About 1 minute before removing chicke from oven, toss rosemary sprigs into skillet. Place chicken, skin side up, on a plate along with rosemary sprigs. Set skillet over medium-high. Cook orange slices just until golden and slightly softened, about 30 seconds per side. Transfer to plate with chicken.

6 Toss chickpeas, olives, and feta with remaining 2 tbsp oil and remaining 1 tbsp lemon juice in a large bowl. Season chickpea salad with salt.

7 Tear open sweet potato and arrange big sections of flesh on a large platter. Place chicken, along with any accumulated juices, around sweet potato, then top with orange slices, chickpea salad and rosemary leaves. Squeeze orange wedges over everything.

Whole Roast Chicken
with Orange-Steamed Beets

436 CALORIES **48G** PROTEIN **19G** FAT **10G** CARBS

SERVES 6

FOR THE CHICKEN

3 lb roaster chicken

4 sprigs thyme

4 bay leaves

4 oregano sprigs

2 tsp kosher salt

1 tsp ground pepper

FOR THE BEETS

2 red beets

1 cup Greek yogurt

1 orange, zested and juiced

2 cups arugula

1 orange, segmented

½ cup feta cheese

1 tsp poppy seeds

CHICKEN

1 With your fingers, loosen the skin from the chicken breast and thigh. Place thyme, bay leaves, and oregano under the skin.

2 Season the chicken with salt and pepper, making sure to get salt in the cavity of the chicken.

3 Preheat oven to 470 degrees. Place a cast iron or roasting pan in the oven and preheat for approximately 10 minutes.

4 Place chicken in pan breast side down. Cook for approximately 15 minutes or until the juices run clear from the breast. Internal temperature should reach 165 degrees.

5 Allow chicken to rest for approximately 10 minutes. Remove herbs and slice.

BEETS

1 Preheat oven to 350 degrees.

2 Place beets on baking sheet and cover with foil. Bake for about 90 minutes. Allow beets to cool then peel and cut into 2-inch chunks.

3 In a mixing bowl add yogurt, orange zest, and juice. Mix well, seasoning with salt and pepper.

4 In a separate bowl add arugula, segmented oranges, and beets. Dress with yogurt dressing.

5 Finish with crumbled feta cheese and poppy seeds. Serve with chicken.

Garlic & Jalapeno Cowboy Ribeye

495	**48**G	**25**G	**6**G
CALORIES	PROTEIN	FAT	CARBS

SERVES 4

¼ cup olive oil

¼ cup balsamic vinegar

2 tbsp mustard

Salt and pepper

24 oz cowboy-cut
   ribeye steak

2 jalapeno peppers,
   halved vertically

2 heads of garlic,
   halved horizontally

2 sprigs basil

1 Make a marinade using the olive oil, balsamic vinegar, mustard, and salt and pepper. Whisk together.

2 Place steak directly in the marinade. Cover in plastic wrap. Refrigerate for 2–6 hours.

3 Pan sear or grill the steak for about 4 minutes on each side, or unt internal temperature reaches 135 degrees.

4 Grill peppers and garlic until golden brown and softened.

5 Garnish with basil.

6 Slice at an angle and serve with roasted peppers and garlic. The garlic should be soft enough to spread like butter.

CHEF'S TIP   Balsamic vinegar, which is vinegar aged from grape must—fresh crushed grape juice including the skins and stems—is a digestive aid, and helps break down proteins. When using it in a marinade as done here, it has the effect of lightly tenderizing the meat. Thus, the longer you allow the meat to marinate the better the results.

LEAD BY EXAMPLE WITH EXERCISE

I want everyone to be able to get up each morning, look in the mirror, and be able to love the person who's looking back at you. Not because you look good by some subjective standard, but because you're proud of the effort you make toward self-improvement every day. As discussed in earlier essays, your kids will follow your example, even subconsciously. Parents who have a healthy love of self are able to raise kids who have a healthy love of self. With regard to health and fitness:

They are a lot less intimidating when you don't have to "pursue" them. When they're a natural part of the flow of your daily life—that's when the magic happens, for you and your kids. If you're going to take the lead for your family in this regard, your journey begins by getting everyone outside on a regular basis. It could be for a walk, a hike, a bike ride, a game of Ultimate Frisbee... it doesn't really matter. What matters is that you get outside and get active together.

I know that some of you reading this will say, "But Robert, I bring my kids to softball and soccer and basketball and..." Wonderful! Keep doing that. It still doesn't take the place of family activity. Why? Because it's not enough to send your kids off to their various activities while you exercise in your own time. You're playing a long game, and in the long game you want to show your kids that exercise is simple, easy, and natural—something that can be done anywhere without special clothing or equipment or driving to a particular place. Because what happens when they lose that?

If, on the other hand, exercise is spontaneous and part of the fabric of everyday life, you'll make yourself and your kids healthier in the process. Best of all, they'll share that value with their kids someday.

Rosemary & Thyme New York Strip

547	**67**G	**28**G	**3**G
CALORIES	PROTEIN	FAT	CARBS

SERVES 2

2 garlic cloves, smashed

3 sprigs thyme

3 sprigs rosemary

3 tbsp soy sauce

2 8 oz New York strip steaks

1 In a mixing bowl add garlic, thyme, rosemary, and soy sauce.

2 Marinate the steak for approximately 24 hours.

3 On a hot grill cook for 8–10 minutes or until internal temperature reaches 125 degrees.

4 Allow to rest for about 10 minutes prior to serving.

Mustard & Dill Chicken
with Steamed Baby Carrots

665	**45G**	**51G**	**9G**
CALORIES	PROTEIN	FAT	CARBS

SERVES 4

FOR THE CHICKEN

¼ cup Dijon mustard

¼ cup white wine vinegar

2 cloves garlic, minced

¼ cup extra virgin
olive oil

4 chicken breasts, skin-on

FOR THE CARROTS

½ cup cilantro

½ cup mint

½ cup parsley

3 cloves garlic

1 tbsp Marcona almonds

½ cup extra virgin
olive oil

1 lemon, juiced and zested

25 baby carrots with tops

1 tsp sesame seeds, toasted

CHICKEN

1 In a mixing bowl, add mustard, vinegar, and minced garlic. Slow
add olive oil, making a vinaigrette.

2 Place chicken breast in the mustard mixture and allow to
marinate for at least 12 hours.

3 Preheat a grill and place chicken breast on the grill. Allow to coo
for about 6 minutes on each side . The chicken should be cooked
to an internal temperature of 165 degrees.

CARROTS

1 In a food processor add cilantro, mint, parsley, garlic, and
Marcona almonds. Puree together and slowly add olive oil
(reserving 1 tsp of olive oil), making a pesto. Finish with
lemon juice, zest, and salt and pepper.

2 Peel carrots and toss with olive oil and salt and pepper

3 Roast carrots in a 400-degree oven, allowing carrots to cook
through, approximately 12 minutes.

4 Cut carrots into 2-inch chunks and toss in pesto, and garnish
with toasted sesame seeds.

Herb-Roasted Chicken

175	**28**G	**7**G	**1**G
CALORIES	PROTEIN	FAT	CARBS

SERVES 4

3 sprigs rosemary

3 sprigs oregano

3 sprigs thyme

1 lemon, zested and juiced

1 tbsp grapeseed oil

2 cloves garlic, minced

1 tsp black pepper

4 chicken breasts, skinless

1 In a food processor add rosemary, oregano, thyme, lemon juice, grapeseed oil, and garlic. Puree.

2 In a mixing bowl add lemon zest, pepper, and chicken breast.

3 Cover chicken with herb mixture and refrigerate.

4 Season chicken breast with salt and place on a hot grill.

5 Cook for about 8 minutes on each side or until chicken has reached an internal temperature of 165 degrees.

Cumin & Curry Chicken

218	**28**G	**10**G	**3**G
CALORIES	PROTEIN	FAT	CARBS

SERVES 2

1 tbsp cumin

1 tbsp curry powder

2 cloves garlic, minced

1 tbsp grapeseed oil

2 chicken breasts, skinless

1 In a mixing bowl add cumin, curry, garlic, and grapeseed oil.

2 Coat the chicken breast with the curry and cumin paste.

3 Allow chicken to marinate for at least 3 hours and up to 24 hours.

4 Season the chicken breast with salt and pepper, and place on a hot grill. Cook for about 5 minutes per side or until the chicken reaches an internal temperature of 165 degrees.

Jamaican Jerk Chicken

387 CALORIES	**43**G PROTEIN	**23**G FAT	**2**G CARBS

SERVES 8

4 limes

4 tsp ground allspice

3 tsp ground nutmeg

3 tsp ground cinnamon

1/8 cup fresh thyme leaves

2 white onions, finely chopped

1 cup chopped scallions

2 Scotch bonnet peppers

2 cups low-sodium soy sauce

12 chicken drumsticks

12 chicken thighs

1 Microwave the limes, one at a time, for 30–60 seconds to extract the oil from the skin. Reserve.

2 Blend the allspice, nutmeg, cinnamon, thyme, onions, scallions, and peppers to make a pulp. Return to the limes and squeeze the juice into the blender; add in the lime oil and soy sauce.

3 Place the chicken and lime skins in a container that you will be able to cover tightly. Pour the marinade over the chicken and let rest in the refrigerator overnight, or a minimum of 4 hours.

4 Cook slowly on a grill or roast in an oven, covered, at 300 degrees for 2 hours. Remove cover and finish cooking for 30 minutes at 400 degrees.

5 Serve with sides. Recommended: coleslaw and roasted butternut squash.

RAISE KIDS THAT WILL NEVER GIVE UP

A young man I know recently told me that he knows what he wants to do with his life. He has the skills to do it and even knows exactly what he needs to do, but he hasn't been able to move forward. He says whenever he tries to focus or attempts to take action, he freezes, unable to pull the trigger. He opined that it might be fear of failure. But he's a talented lad. I think he knows deep down that if he puts his mind to anything, he can't possibly fail.

But knowing exactly what you need to do doesn't make doing it any easier. Expectation of success can paralyze you just as effectively as expectation of failure. So what's the problem?

In all my travels and interactions with some very wildly successful people at the very top of their professions, I've learned that there is a third fear—between the fear of failure and the fear of success—that can afflict even the best of us. It's the fear of mediocrity.

Mediocrity sits perfectly between success and failure. Unlike pure failure where you get no part of what you want, you succeed partially: You get the job or the promotion or whatever it might be, but you don't excel. You're never truly great at it because you just can't bring yourself to take real action. You don't take any creative risks because you're worried it won't have the kind of impact on the world that you secretly hope for.

In such a scenario, inaction becomes your only method of perceived self-preservation. You'll never know if your actions will have relatively little impact if you can't bring yourself to take action in the first place. You don't even realize you're sabotaging yourself, yet that's exactly what's happening. Finally, you realize too late that inaction is the only true form of failure.

I have no tolerance for inaction. We only really learn by doing, so you can't learn if you're not doing. I couldn't possibly begin to tell you how many recipes I've screwed up or meals I've ruined over the years. What I can tell you is the lessons learned from the screw-ups are what made me who I am. Had I been too timid to reach above my station, to try to be great—and to risk humiliation in the process—there isn't a snowball's chance in hell that you would have ever heard of me.

This is a lesson you absolutely must impart to your children. It's OK to get confused, or stuck in a rut, or scared. These are all part of the human condition. We don't always have control over the feelings of joy or fear that come and go. But we always have control over how we react to them. Taking action is what you need to do. That can be in the form of cooking, exercising, journaling or any of a thousand other productive endeavors. Falling idle and brooding over your misfortune does nothing but create more misfortune. Bad things are going to happen. How long will they bog you down and set you on a path apart from your dreams? Only you get to answer that.

Lead a life that demonstrates to your children the tremendous upside of continually taking calculated risks—and showing them the healthy, constructive way to deal with disappointments and setbacks. Show them that mediocrity can't come for someone one who refuses to give up.

Show your kids that you are in control and you'll have kids that know how to take control.

Rosemary & Garlic Pork Loin

308 CALORIES	**30**G PROTEIN	**20**G FAT	**0**G CARBS

SERVES 4

3 cloves garlic

2 sprigs rosemary, chopped

1 cup Dijon mustard

1 tbsp fennel seeds, roughly chopped

1 tbsp cumin

2 tbsp extra virgin olive oil

2 tbsp grapeseed oil

1 ½ lb pork loin

1 In a food processor add garlic, rosemary, Dijon mustard, fennel seeds, cumin, olive oil, and grapeseed oil and puree.

2 Coat pork loin with mustard and herb mixture.

3 Place pork loin in a 400-degree oven for 30 minutes.

4 Drop the oven temperature to 325 degrees and cook for another 45 minutes.

5 When the internal temperature reaches 135 degrees, allow to rest for approximately 15 minutes prior to serving.

Simple Tomato Sauce

308 CALORIES   **30**G PROTEIN   **20**G FAT   **0**G CARBS

SERVES 6

16 oz canned plum tomatoes

3 tbsp grapeseed oil

2 Spanish white onions, medium dice

3 cloves garlic, minced

3 tbsp tomato paste

3 tbsp red wine

1 bunch basil, torn by hand

1 Place tomatoes in a mixing bowl. Crush with your hands.

2 In a medium sauce pot, add oil, onions, and garlic. Allow to cook over medium heat for about 8 minutes. Add tomato paste and allow to cook for 3 minutes. Add red wine allow to cook for another 4 minutes. Add crushed tomatoes. Season with salt and pepper.

3 Allow sauce to simmer for 1 hour.

4 Last add torn basil and taste for seasoning before serving.

GET THE KIDS INVOLVED   Crushing tomatoes with your hands is a dirty job—which little kids absolutely love! Plus there's no better way to get to "know" your food than by rolling up your sleeves and transforming it with your bare hands.

Meatballs

451 CALORIES	**46**G PROTEIN	**22**G FAT	**15**G CARBS

SERVES 6

- 1 Spanish white onion
- 3 cloves garlic, minced
- 3 cups diced bread, like a baguette
- 2 large eggs
- ½ cup ricotta cheese
- ½ cup Parmesan cheese
- 1 lb ground pork
- 1 lb ground veal
- 2 tbsp extra virgin olive oil
- 1 tbsp Italian parsley, chopped
- 1 tbsp oregano, chopped
- 2 tbsp grapeseed oil
- 3 cups basic tomato sauce

1 In a small saucepan over medium heat, sweat onion and garlic.

2 In a large bowl, soak bread in a water for a couple minutes. Stra[ ] out excess liquid.

3 In a separate large bowl, add eggs, ricotta cheese, Parmesan cheese, and onion and garlic mixture. Add ground meat, soaked bread, extra virgin olive oil, parsley, and oregano. Mix thorough[ ]

4 In a large sauté pan over high heat, brown meatballs in grapese[ ] oil on all sides.

5 Once balls have been browned, place them in a separate sauce p[ ] with basic tomato sauce. Bring to a simmer and finish cooking, approximately 1 hour.

Bucatini all'Amatriciana

394	**21**G	**14**G	**46**G
CALORIES	PROTEIN	FAT	CARBS

SERVES 6

1 lb bucatini pasta

1 cup bacon

2 cups crushed tomatoes

1 tbsp butter

1 tsp chili flakes

1 cup Parmesan cheese

1 bunch basil

1 Fill a large pot with water. Add salt so it is well-seasoned and bring to a boil over high heat. Add pasta and allow to cook for 2 minutes, making sure it doesn't stick together. Cook for approximately 10 minutes or until slightly al dente.

2 In a medium saucepan over high heat, add bacon to render, approximately 5 minutes.

3 Next add tomatoes and allow to simmer. Add bucatini and bring back to a simmer.

4 Remove pasta from heat. Finish by adding butter, chili flakes, and cheese

5 Tear basil with your hands and garnish on top of pasta.

CONQUER THE FEAR OF MAKING MISTAKES

Fear is OK. Fear of making mistakes is not.

If you were to take stock of every element of your life and ask yourself if you have made the absolute most of every opportunity you have, there's a good chance you'd have to say no. At least if you're being honest. No one can go full throttle all the time. Our performance as employees, parents, and spouses tends to ebb and flow. We're firing on all cylinders one minute, then we're mired in a rough patch, unable to do more than the bare minimum required to get by after we drag ourselves out of bed in the morning.

I don't believe it's possible to eliminate the latter, but it can be minimized. You can relegate the times you're "off" to the times of your choosing, like vacation, or the times you have no control over, like when you're sick or injured.

We all might have one or more temporary factors holding us back from reaching our full potential. But I believe by eliminating just one factor—the fear of making mistakes—you can begin the process of optimizing your life. Sometimes called analysis paralysis, the fear of making mistakes holds us back from doing anything. We look at all that could go wrong and let it stop us dead in our tracks. Of all the things that could hold you back, I find this fear to be the most insidious, primarily because no matter what your endeavor, you could choose to focus on potential downsides or pitfalls along the way. Likewise, it is a choice to instead focus your attention on all that could go right. It's up to you. Fears of one flavor or another are always going to pop into your head. How long they stay is entirely your decision.

THE PROCESS IS PROGRESS.

A lot of big, successful bands have taken to releasing early demos of famous songs in recent years. Everyone from The Beatles to Metallica have decided to show fans that the songs they love—the ones stuck in their head for years—didn't always sound like the finished products they became. When the band Soundgarden remastered its hit album *Superunknown* for its 20th anniversary a couple of years ago, frontman Chris Cornell said at the time that fans could expect to hear "a lot of embarrassing stuff."

To me, these music demos are one of the most encouraging gifts I've ever received—as a writer, a chef, a TV personality, a businessman, a husband, and a father. When you hear that an early demo of a huge, megahit song once only contained a small germ of an idea and that it needed to be reworked for countless hours, it reminds you that only by continuing to grind and embrace mistakes along the way can you create something truly special.

That's the case whether you're talking about a making a new recipe, trying a new fitness routine, or strengthening a bond with a loved one. No matter what you're trying to accomplish, you're going to make mistakes, so you might as well pick a direction and run. The only way to truly fail is to sit on your hands and do nothing, too worried about all that might go wrong.

> The only way to truly fail is to sit on your hands and do nothing, too worried about all that might go wrong.

133

Cider-Brined Fried Chicken

308 CALORIES

30G PROTEIN

20G FAT

0G CARBS

SERVES 8

3 tbsp kosher salt, divided

3 tbsp pepper, divided

2 cups apple cider vinegar

1 cup apple juice

4 cups all-purpose flour

4 cups vegetable oil

8 pieces chicken, legs and thighs

1 Mix 2 tbsp salt, 2 tbsp pepper, 4 cups water, vinegar, and apple juice in a 2 gallon container. Add the chicken and allow to marinate for 30 minutes up to 3 hours in the refrigerator.

2 Add the remaining 1 tbsp salt and 1 tbsp pepper to the flour, mix well, and hold until ready to fry.

3 In a cast iron skillet, add the oil and bring to 350 degrees over high heat. Remove the chicken from the brine, pat dry with a paper towel, and dredge the chicken in the seasoned flour, coatir well and tapping off any excess. Once all the chicken is floured, add to the oil, in batches, and cook until golden brown on both sides, 8–9 minutes per side. The internal temperature must be 165 degrees to be cooked thoroughly. Drain thoroughly on paper towels before serving.

BBQ-Glazed Chicken Nuggets

523 CALORIES	**27**G PROTEIN	**12**G FAT	**60**G CARBS

SERVES 6

BBQ GLAZE

¼ cup apple cider vinegar

1 tsp garlic powder

1 tsp onion powder

2 tsp chili powder

¼ cup Worcestershire sauce

1 cup ketchup

¼ cup molasses

¼ cup packed dark brown sugar

¼ cup honey

CHICKEN NUGGETS

2 cups all-purpose flour

½ teaspoon salt

¼ teaspoon pepper

2 8 oz boneless chicken breasts, cut into pieces

¼ cup olive oil

1 Prepare the BBQ glaze. Pour apple cider vinegar into a small saucepan and whisk in garlic powder, onion powder, and chili powder. Bring to a boil and add Worcestershire sauce, ketchup, molasses, dark brown sugar, and honey. Lower heat to medium or medium low and allow to bubble and thicken.

2 Preheat oven to 425 degrees. In a plastic bag, shake together flour, salt and pepper, and add chicken pieces in batches to coat.

3 Place chicken pieces on a baking sheet (lined with heavy duty foil for easy cleanup) and drizzle olive oil over. Bake for about 15 minutes, and then coat each piece with some of the glaze and bake for 5–10 more minutes. You can do a second coat of glaze for the last 5 minutes, or serve any additional glaze on the side.

GET THE KIDS INVOLVED   Most of this recipe can be done by kids of any age with just a little bit of parental guidance. They'll have fun combining the glaze ingredients, shaking the chicken pieces in the bag, and glazing the finished product. Plus, the fact that every kid loves chicken nuggets should certainly pique their interest!

Pulled Pork Sandwiches

WITH ROLL

| **448** CALORIES | **42G** PROTEIN | **13G** FAT | **38G** CARBS |

SERVES 6

1.5 lbs pork shoulder

2–3 whole cloves

2 tbsp smoked paprika or smokey spice rub of your choice

1 red onion, sliced thin

1 cup water

6 oz BBQ sauce

1 Stud pork with cloves and rub with seasoning blend.

2 Place roast in crock pot or slow cooker and top with onions. Cover pork with water and slow cook for 8–10 hours.

3 Remove pork, discard cloves, then drain fat and water. Allow pork to cool, then shred by hand or with fork.

4 Return meat to pot and add BBQ sauce. Heat for 1–2 hours. Serve straight up or on a roll.

GET THE KIDS INVOLVED There's no right or wrong way to shred the cooked pork, so put the kids to work! They can use their hands or a pair of forks Bear Paws—available at Amazon and other retailers—are probably the easiest way to do it. The standard set is a bit sharp (though you can opt for plastic ones but provide easy-to-use handles and a fun shape that kids definitely appreciate.

Grilled Chicken Cacciatore

539 CALORIES

48G PROTEIN

20G FAT

40G CARBS

SERVES 6

¼ cup olive oil

3 medium onions, sliced

4 green bell peppers, julienned

4 red bell peppers, julienned

3 cups white mushrooms, cleaned and quartered

6 large ripe tomatoes, large dice

2 tbsp tomato paste

2 cups tomato juice

3 tbsp chopped shallots

3 tbsp chopped garlic

1 cup fresh basil leaves, chopped

1 cup fresh parsley leaves, chopped

Salt and pepper

12 4 oz boneless chicken breasts

FOR THE POLENTA

1 large onion, chopped

6 tbsp butter

8 cups water

2 cups yellow cornmeal

Grated Parmesan

1 Heat oil in a large saucepot and sauté onions, peppers, and mushrooms until onions begin to turn translucent and peppers begin to soften.

2 Add tomatoes, tomato paste, tomato juice, shallots, garlic, basil, and parsley. Season with salt and pepper. Let simmer 45 minutes until medium thickness.

3 Preheat a grill to high.

4 Season chicken breasts with salt and pepper. Grill on both sides until cooked through.

POLENTA:

1 Saute onion in butter until softened. Add water and stir in cornmeal. Cook on low heat, stirring often, for about 40 minutes until tender. Sprinkle with Parmesan.

2 Arrange on serving platter and spoon sauce around. Serve with a side of polenta (as you would mashed potatoes) and remaining sauce in a gravy boat.

Colorado Lamb Chops
with Warm Buckwheat Salad & Tzatziki Sauce

795	**66**G	**51**G	**17**G
CALORIES	PROTEIN	FAT	CARBS

SERVES 6

FOR THE RACK OF LAMB

1 lamb rack

Salt and pepper

FOR THE BUCKWHEAT SALAD

1 tbsp grapeseed oil

½ cup cauliflower

2 tbsp cashews, lightly toasted and crushed

1 tbsp curry powder

2 tbsp olives, chopped

2 tbsp capers, chopped

2 tbsp golden raisins, softened in hot water

1 Calabrian chili, thinly sliced

1 cup buckwheat

1 tbsp parsley, chopped

TZATZIKI SAUCE

1 cup cucumber, grated

2 cups Greek yogurt

1 cup sour cream

1 shallot, minced

2 cloves garlic, minced

2 tbsp lemon juice

2 tbsp olive oil

2 tbsp dill, chopped

1 Preheat oven to 350 degrees.

2 Season lamb rack with salt and pepper, and sear in pan over high heat. Place rack in a rimmed baking sheet and then roast in oven, about 20–25 minutes, bringing internal temperature t 130 degrees. Let rack rest for at least 5 minutes prior to serving

3 In a sauté pan, heat grapeseed oil. Add cauliflower and cook fo approximately 2 minutes, allowing cauliflower to get some colo on it. Add cashews and curry powder, and cook for about anotl er 2 minutes.

4 Add olives, capers, raisins, chili, and buckwheat. Cook for another 2 minutes off the heat. Add parsley and mix together.

TZATZIKI

1 In a small bowl add cucumber and season with salt. Allow to si for 20 minutes, and strain off any additional liquid.

2 Add yogurt, sour cream, shallots, garlic, lemon juice, olive oil, and dill.

3 Season with salt and pepper.

SCHEDULE TIME FOR FUN

Families with busy schedules have learned to live life by the calendar. Whether that's a shared virtual calendar or an old-fashioned paper calendar hanging on the fridge, it's the only way to keep track of everything from work to school hours to everyone's myriad extracurricular activities. It helps keep track of meals, too; the surest way to get into an effective rhythm is to repeat meals that everyone likes and are easy to make. Taco Tuesday and Pizza Friday didn't happen by accident. They happened because we're creatures of habit and it makes life a whole lot easier to repeat what is successful.

I strongly encourage everyone to keep a calendar with their families. I share my

own personal calendar with my whole staff and family; it's the only practical way to keep them apprised of my movements when I travel about 300 days a year.

When I first started keeping a calendar I learned that it made me more efficient, but I soon realized that I wasn't scheduling any time to just kick back and enjoy myself. I'm the type of person that wants to make the most of every opportunity, so I maxed myself out. If there was a gap in my schedule and someone wanted to hire me for an appearance or film a segment, I jumped at the opportunity. In my head I was maximizing my career and being productive. While true, it came to the detriment of other areas of my life. Never mind vacations, I wasn't even scheduling days off. This is a terrible habit. Planning ahead for time to have fun isn't just important, it's absolutely essential. Without time to recharge and have a laugh, you're missing the point of life—not to mention actively making yourself worse at the stuff you're trying to accomplish!

Burnout comes for all who push too hard and too fast for too long. This can become the case with your family, too, if you only focus on work and school and practice and lessons.

You don't need money to plan an extravagant vacation (though getting away when you can is helpful). But at least once a month you should plan a day when you and your family can just be yourselves. Hike a nearby trail you've never been to. Plan a trip to your local historical society and learn more about where you live. Or just light a fire in the backyard, make s'mores, and tell stories to one another.

I've been all around the world with Gail, Annalise, and Talia, but some of our very best memories have come at moments such as these.

Spiced Short Rib

722 CALORIES **79**G PROTEIN **41**G FAT **6**G CARBS

SERVES 4

5 short ribs

RUB

1 tbsp grated nutmeg

1 tsp cinnamon

1 tbsp kosher salt

1 tsp black pepper

BRAISING LIQUID

2 carrots

1 whole onions

2 ribs celery

1 quarts red wine

2 qts beef stock
(chicken stock is a
suitable substitute)

SACHET

4 bay leaves

4 sprigs thyme

2 sprigs rosemary

1 tbsp peppercorns

1 tsp allspice

1 Combine all the ingredients for the rub and put the ribs in the re frigerator to cure for around 12 hours. If you don't have that long 4–6 hours is also OK.

2 Remove the ribs from the fridge and sear in a roasting pan over medium-high heat on the stove. Be sure to sear the ribs on all sides and get a fair amount of color.

3 While the ribs are cooking, large dice the carrots, onions, and celery.

4 Once all the ribs have been seared, turn the heat down to mediu and add the carrots, celery, and onions. Cook until softened and has taken on some color, this should take about 20–25 minutes.

5 With the vegetable still in the pan add the red wine and deglaze. Turn the heat up to high and be sure to remove any fond stuck t the bottom of the pan.

6 Once the wine has almost completely reduced, add the beef stoc Add the beef ribs back to the pan, cover completely with water, and add your sachet. If the ribs do not fit in the roaster complete ly covered with braising liquid, place into two smaller vessels.

7 Bring the roasting pan back to a simmer and cover with parch-ment first and then foil.

8 Place in the oven to braise for 5 hours at 250 degrees. Check to make sure the ribs are done before removing from the oven. If necessary, continue to cook, checking periodically until the meat begins to fall off the bone.

Fish & Chips

579	**51**G	**15**G	**60**G
CALORIES	PROTEIN	FAT	CARBS

SERVES 4

BATTER & FISH
16 oz pilsner-style beer

½ cup water

1 tbsp baking powder

2 lbs all-purpose flour

1 whole lemon

½ cup rice flour

4 8 oz portions of white
  fish like cod or haddock

5 cups shoe-string
  French fries

2 tbsp rendered bacon

SEASONED FLOUR
2 cups all-purpose flour

Lemon zest

Salt and black pepper

CURRY AIOLI
1 cup mayonnaise

1 tbsp yellow curry powder

½ tbsp turmeric

2 tbsp malt vinegar

2 tbsp honey

Salt and pepper

1 In a large bowl add beer, water, and whisk in baking powder, lemon zest, rice flour, and all-purpose flour.

2 In a large mixing bowl add flour, lemon zest, and salt and pepper to make seasoned flour. Dredge fish in flour.

3 Take fish from seasoned flour, making sure to shake off excess.

4 Place fish in beer batter, coating the entire fish.

5 Place fish in a 350-degree fryer using a pair of tongs. Allow to cook for approximately 5–7 minutes, making sure to flip the fish half way through the cooking process.

6 When fish is done, add French fries and allow to cook for approximately 4 minutes.

7 To make curry aioli, combine mayo, curry powder, turmeric, vinegar, honey, and salt and pepper in a small bowl until smooth.

8 Serve with curry aioli and rendered bacon.

CHEF'S TIP A classic, simple British pub food, fish and chips are easily elevated with the curry aioli. If curry's not your thing, make a simple aioli instead: Combine 1 egg yolk, 2 tbsp grapeseed oil, 1 tsp lemon juice, salt and pepper, and mix it in a blender. For a little more pop, add two garlic cloves to the blender.

Brined Pork Chops
with Apple Hash

511 CALORIES   **48G** PROTEIN   **27G** FAT   **17G** CARBS

SERVES 6

8 cups water

1 lemon, juiced

1 lime, juiced

1 orange, juiced

¼ cup fennel sprigs

2 tbsp kosher or sea salt

6 8–10 oz bone-in pork chops

4 tbsp grapeseed oil

2 cups Yukon Gold potatoes, thinly sliced

1 cup red onion, thinly sliced

1 tsp salt

1 tsp white pepper

2 cups Granny Smith apple, thinly sliced

1 tsp sriracha

1 Mix 8 cups water, fruit juices, fennel, and 2 tbsp kosher or sea salt in a large saucepan over medium heat. Simmer for 10 minutes. After heating, remove and allow to cool. Add the chops to the brine and refrigerate for 3 to 24 hours.

2 In a large sauté pan over high heat, add 2 tbsp oil, then add 3 chops to the pan. Reduce heat and cook 6–7 minutes per side, which should yield a golden-brown pork chop. Repeat the process for the remaining 3 chops. Hold warm until serving.

3 Return pan to medium-high heat, add 2 tbsp oil, allow it to warm, then add potatoes. Stir until potatoes brown on the edges. Add onions, salt, and white pepper, and cook until onions soften. Reduce heat to medium, add apples, and cook for 4 minutes. Add hash to the plate, top with pork chops and sriracha.

Turkey Pot Pie

421	**40**G	**17**G	**26**G
CALORIES	PROTEIN	FAT	CARBS

SERVES 4

2 tbsp butter

1 Spanish white onion, chopped

2 celery ribs, medium dice

3 carrots, small dice

4 tbsp all-purpose flour

4 cups turkey stock (or leftover gravy)

2 potatoes, peeled and medium dice

3 cups cooked and shredded turkey (dark meat preferred)

2 tbsp tarragon and parsley, chopped

1 square prepared puff pastry square

1 egg, beaten

1 Preheat oven to 375 degrees.

2 In a medium sauce pot, melt butter, add diced onion, and allow to sweat for 4 minutes. Add celery and carrots, and allow to cook for another 4–5 minutes.

3 Add turkey and allow to cook for 4 minutes. Add tarragon and parsley.

4 Add all-purpose flour and allow to cook for 4 minutes.

5 Add stock and bring to a simmer. Add potatoes, turkey, and herbs; simmer until fork tender.

6 Brush the pastry with egg wash.

7 Bake pie for 20–30 minutes or until crust is golden brown.

CHEF'S TIP   One of my all-time favorite comfort foods, pot pies are a real treat, especially in the fall and winter (try making this with your Thanksgiving leftovers). The crust, combined with a rich broth to infuse flavor to the veggies, are a great way to get kids to broaden their palates.

MAKE NEW YEAR'S RESOLUTIONS—AT ANY TIME OF YEAR

Statistics on the failure of New Year's resolutions are absolutely staggering. One study showed that just 8% of people realize their goals.

Fitness goals in particular are abandoned with blinding speed, with a majority of January newcomers throwing in the towel before the month is even over.

a week and all of a sudden you need to skip a day or two because of work or a family emergency, are you going to let that setback derail your entire program? Most people would, because both action and inaction are backed by a powerful force called inertia.

I wrote about this concept of inertia in my book *Fit Fuel*: Action begets more action, laziness begets more laziness. Take the example of any super-successful person. They're able to stay on top because they ride the wave. If they're smarter than the average person, it's only because they're smart enough not to let go of inertia. Once you're in the habit of success, it takes more than one misstep to fall out of the habit. Now take the example of somone who can't get off the couch. Inertia is at play in this experience as well. Unfortunately for the person who can't get their life together, the same holds true; inertia is hard to reverse.

The good news in the above example is this: You can start to form new habits and build your own inertia in as little as three weeks. Some studies suggest it's longer than that, but in my personal experience, three weeks is a major hurdle. Power through that benchmark and you're on your way. At the three-week mark, you've built serious inertia, the kind where it will feel worse to stop than it will to continue.

You can make a major change in your life starting right now. It doesn't matter what month of the year it is. Just remember that the act of summoning the raw willpower to make the change is a bigger challenge in the beginning. Soon, healthier or more productive habits will be part of the new you. Just be prepared to say goodbye to the old you.

Why does this happen? Because intention, in and of itself, can feel powerful in the moment. Everyone who makes a New Year's resolution sincerely wants to see it come true. When they say they will change, they believe it. But no matter how pure an intention you have, that intention loses all of its power over time if you lack a clear plan of action to back it up. But more than just a solid workout and nutrition plan, you need to have a plan to deal with adversity. If your new plan has you going to the gym five days

Crab Salad Sliders

377	**26**G	**16**G	**45**G
CALORIES	PROTEIN	FAT	CARBS

SERVES 4

1 lb lump crab meat

¼ cup mayonnaise

¼ cup plain Greek yogurt

1 cucumber, small dice

1 fennel bulb, small dice

1 tbsp dill, chopped

1 tbsp tarragon, chopped

1 lemon, juiced and zested

2 cloves garlic, minced

4 large Bibb lettuce leaves

1 beefsteak tomato, sliced

4 small brioche buns,
  toasted

1 In a large bowl mix all ingredients together except lettuce, tomato
and buns.

2 Serve on toasted bun with lettuce and tomato.

CHEF'S TIP   Lump crab meat hard to come by where you are? No sweat. You
can swap out the crab meat with canned tuna or grilled and diced shrimp, leaving every other ingredient in the recipe the same.

Shepherd's Pie

524 CALORIES

30G PROTEIN

28G FAT

37G CARBS

SERVES 5

1 tbsp olive oil

1 onion, diced

1 clove garlic, crushed

1 large carrot, diced

1 lb lamb, minced

1 cup beef stock

1 lb tomatoes, chopped

3 tbsp tomato puree

1 tbsp corn flour

2 lbs potatoes

1 stick butter

Salt and pepper

1 Heat the olive oil in a pan over medium heat. Add the onion, garlic, and carrot and cook until soft. Add the lamb and beef stock, and cook until the meat is brown and has a crumbly texture. Stir in the tomatoes, tomato puree, and corn flour. Simmer, stirring occasionally, for about 15 minutes or until thickened.

2 Peel and chop the potatoes, toss in a large pot and cover with water. Bring to a boil over medium heat and cook until soft. Drain and add them back to the pot. Mash with a potato masher, stir in the butter, and season to taste with salt and pepper.

3 Set broiler to low.

4 Put the filling into a deep baking dish, top with mashed potatoes and put under the broiler until the top is brown and crisp.

Chicken Masala

492 CALORIES

26G PROTEIN

25G FAT

24G CARBS

SERVES 4

4 boneless, skinless
  chicken breasts,
  cut into cubes

1 lemon, juiced

1 onion, quartered

2 garlic cloves, peeled

1 garlic clove, thinly sliced

1 2-inch chunk ginger,
  peeled

1 ½ cups plain, nonfat
  Greek yogurt

½ cup olive oil

Garam masala paste

1 sprig parsley

1 In a bowl, toss the chicken with the lemon juice.

2 Place the quartered onion, 2 cloves garlic, and ginger in a food processor and chop finely.

3 Add the yogurt and strain the lemon juice from the chicken into the processor. Puree until blended, then pour back over the chicken. Cover and marinate in fridge for 24 hours.

4 Thread the chicken onto kebab skewers, reserving the marinade. Barbecue or grill as slowly as possible until just cooked through, 6–8 minutes; it's very important not to overcook the chicken. Remove the chicken from the skewers.

5 Meanwhile, make the masala. Heat olive oil in a wok. Add chopped onion and thinly sliced garlic. Fry for 4 minutes until soft. Mix in 3 tbsp masala paste, 1 tbsp at a time, and stir-fry mixture for 2–3 minutes until fragrant. Add the reserved yogurt marinade. Mix and bring to a boil. Add chicken and cook for 3 minutes.

6 Garnish with chopped parsley and serve hot over a half cup of spiced basmati rice.

BBQ St. Louis Ribs

594	**35**G	**36**G	**29**G
CALORIES	PROTEIN	FAT	CARBS

SERVES 12

FOR THE BBQ SAUCE

2 cups ketchup

2 cups apple cider vinegar

1 cup Dijon mustard

1 cup brown sugar

2 tbsp cayenne pepper

2 tbsp kosher salt

1 tbsp black pepper

FOR THE SPICE RUB

½ cup kosher salt

¼ cup ground mustard

¼ cup paprika

¼ cup black pepper

¼ cup cayenne pepper

¼ cup ground
white pepper

¼ cup seafood seasoning

2 tbsp ground cumin

RIBS

4 full racks St. Louis ribs

1 Make the sauce. Mix the ketchup, vinegar, Dijon mustard, brown sugar, cayenne pepper, and salt and black pepper in a bowl. Transfer to a thick-bottomed saucepot over medium-low heat. Allow the sauce to warm and mix over the heat for 10–15 minutes, stirring throughout. Remove and cool.

2 Make the spice rub. In a bowl, mix the salt, ground mustard, paprika, black pepper, cayenne pepper, white pepper, seafood seasoning, and cumin together with a spoon. After mixing, keep dry and covered.

3 Prep the ribs. Remove the silver skin from the bottom side of the ribs. Then evenly rub each rack with ¼ cup of the spice rub on top and bottom. Wrap each rack in plastic wrap and keep overnight in the refrigerator or cooler.

4 Heat a smoker with pecan or other fruit wood, bringing it to 165 degrees and maintaining temperature. Once the temperature is obtained, remove the plastic and place the ribs in the smoker for 4 hours, keeping for doneness at this point. The ribs should be cooked, but not falling off the bone.

5 Remove the ribs from the smoker and glaze each rack with ½ cup of the BBQ sauce. Then return to the smoker for 30–40 minutes. Again, remove and glaze with additional ½ cup sauce and finish for a final 20 minutes. After the second glaze and final cooking, remove the ribs from the smoker. Allow to rest for 5 minutes, and then cut into single or double bone sections and serve.

ALWAYS FOCUS ON THE POSITIVE

For kids, it's too easy for healthy changes to start to feel like drudgery. There's a pretty good chance that asking your family to put away their phones, cook a healthy meal together, and to get out and exercise has turned you into an enemy. Everyone just wants to chill and there you are forcing them to do a bunch of crap they really have no interest in. If they don't outright rebel, they go through the motions without any enthusiasm, which is almost as bad. If it comes to this, you're done. Give up now and start from scratch at a later date.

Forcing anyone, even very young kids, to do your bidding is a tactic that is destined to fail. You might get your way in the short-term, but in the long-term, they will hate you for it and grow to hate your underlying message. And yes, I know that all kids rebel at some stage, but do you really want sedentary habits punctuated with smartphone and fast food addiction to be part of their rebellious phase? It'll happen if you try to force healthy habits down their throats.

In the meal planning essay on page 26 I offered a simple dialogue to follow so that you can gently coax your kids into giving up their phones for dinnertime. There's nothing underhanded about it; it's just a spoonful of sugar to help the medicine go down. You'll want to employ similar tactics along the way to help your family stay the course. If you don't put in the work to keep them positive about the changes you're making, and if you start using phrases like, "Because I said so," then you're on your way to becoming a drill sergeant. Stop and reassess your approach.

In general, your kids will respond to the positive vibe you put out. (They also won't have any tolerance for a hypocrite—nor should they—so that means no sneaking any glances at your phone during the dinner hours, either.) Here are a few ways to keep the whole family positive.

MIND YOUR LANGUAGE

When you describe cooking, say things like, "I'm really excited to show you what this blender does to a cucumber in just a few seconds," or "Wait till you see what happens to the short ribs when they hit the hot pan. It's incredible." They may not think it's so incredible, but your enthusiasm, or lack thereof, will eventually take root in their collective psyche. When describing the meal itself, use words like "delicious" and "fresh" and remind them that "you can't get a meal this good at a restaurant." Same goes for exercise. Emphasize the fact that you are actually *acquiring energy*, not *doing work*. The more you show genuine enthusiasm and the less you say things like, "Well, we have to do this together," or "But you promised you'd do this for me," the smoother your sailing will be.

HANG OUT WITH LIKE-MINDED PEOPLE

Ironically, social media—and Facebook in particular—makes it easier than ever to find like-minded folks. Look for parenting groups in your town. Join up and write a brief post introducing yourself. You could

say something like, *"Hi everyone! Thanks for having me in this group. I'm currently trying to get my family into healthier habits. We cook a meal together at least one night per week and go for a light walk after dinner. We've even banned phones during dinner once everyone's home from school and work! So far so good, but I'd love to widen the circle a bit to reinforce these habits with my kids. Would anyone want to get together with their kids for a healthy barbecue at the park and maybe play a game of kickball afterward? I'll bring the food; only rule is no phones allowed. Let me know! Thanks!"* Showing your kids that other families do similar things will go a long way toward normalizing the behavior and making it a lifelong habit.

VISUALIZE SUCCESS

What does the ideal picture of success look like for you? Visualize it every morning when you wake up and every night before you go to sleep. Imagine everyone pitching in to cook, devouring a healthy dinner together, and having fun afterward—all distraction-free. Write down exactly what you want on an index card and keep it in your wallet or purse. It could be as simple as, "I never want my kids to have to struggle with their weight," or "I want my spouse and my kids to love their bodies," or "I want my kids to love life, not waste time on their phones."

Keep the reasons why you're doing this close at hand and you'll stay motivated and disciplined. If you want to be a bit bolder, print them out in big font and hang them on the fridge. It's also never too early to encourage your kids to do the same. Encourage them to write down their ultimate dreams. Ask them what they want to be when they grow up and where they want to live. Remind them that nothing is impossible and not to hold back when they write down their dreams. It might seem hard to believe, but no matter how old they are, they can subconsciously start taking steps to make those dreams a reality.

IV
DESSERTS

WHEN IT'S TIME FOR A SWEET REWARD, DON'T
REACH FOR STORE-BOUGHT COOKIES AND
CANDY. COOK UP SOMETHING TRULY
WORTHY OF THE EXTRA CALORIES.

Oatmeal Cookies

| **258** CALORIES | **5G** PROTEIN | **10G** FAT | **38G** CARBS |

SERVES 8

½ cup whole wheat flour

½ cup all-purpose flour

1 tsp baking powder

⅓ cup vegetable oil

⅔ cup packed
   dark brown sugar

1 large egg

1 tsp pure vanilla extract

½ cup rolled oats

½ cup dried currants
   or raisins

1 Preheat oven to 350 degrees.

2 In a medium bowl, whisk together flours and baking powder; set aside. In a large bowl, whisk together oil, sugar, egg, and vanilla. Add flour mixture and stir to combine. Mix in oats and currants.

3 Using 2 tbsp of dough per cookie, roll into balls. Place on two baking sheets lined with parchment paper, 1 ½ inches apart.

4 Bake until lightly browned, 15–17 minutes, rotating sheets halfway through.

5 Cool 5 minutes on sheets, then transfer cookies to a wire rack to cool completely.

GET THE KIDS INVOLVED Scooping cookie dough and rolling it into balls is a task tailor-made for little hands. They'll get a kick out of getting their hands dirty and being largely responsible for the look of the finished product.

Old-Fashioned Hot Chocolate

583 **CALORIES** **11G** **PROTEIN** **36G** **FAT** **54G** **CARBS**

SERVES 4

3 cups whole milk

3 tbsp granulated sugar

3 cinnamon sticks

10 oz semi-sweet chocolate, finely chopped

Marshmallows

1 In a small sauce pot, add milk, sugar, and cinnamon bring to a simmer.

2 Using a whisk add chocolate.

3 Strain, serve in mugs and top with marshmallows. Drizzle melte chocolate over top if desired.

CHEF'S TIP Stay vigilant with this recipe; letting the milk sit on heat withou continuous whisking invites the milk and chocolate to stick to the bottom of th pot, which is notoriously difficult to clean up. Not to mention you'll wind up wi a subtle (or not so subtle) burnt flavor in the finished product.

Fudge Brownies

462	**6**G	**27**G	**56**G
CALORIES	PROTEIN	FAT	CARBS

SERVES 8

4 whole eggs

²/₃ cup sugar

2 cups semi-sweet
  chocolate chips

1 stick butter

1 cup all-purpose flour

1 tsp salt

1 Preheat oven to 350 degrees.

2 Beat eggs and add sugar until combined. Do not overmix.

3 Melt the chocolate chips and butter in a small saucepan. Allow to cool slightly.

4 Slowly temper: Add small amounts of the chocolate-butter mixture to the eggs so that the eggs do not scramble. Continue until all of the chocolate-butter mixture is combined with the egg-sugar mixture.

5 Slowly incorporate flour; avoid overmixing, but being sure to break up lumps.

6 Add salt.

7 Line a baking tray with foil and parchment paper.

8 Bake for 12 minutes. Allow to cool slightly before serving.

SPREAD LOVE ON SOCIAL MEDIA

I believe family time is sacred. I also believe that we can enjoy everything in moderation. With that in mind, you should know I'm not some anti-technology extremist. Quite the opposite. Not a day goes by where I'm not posting something to Facebook, Instagram, or Twitter. I love interacting with fans and there's never been a better time in history for ease of communication between public figures and the general public. Rest in peace, fan mail.

Social media is also a wonderful tool to keep old classmates and friends connected. Casual acquaintances and old colleagues usually fade from memory with time, but now that almost never happens. You probably know someone you worked with for one month five years ago who is on your timeline liking pictures and commenting on everything you post. Depending on how you look at that, it's a miracle or a curse. Either way, technologies that didn't exist just a few short years ago have fundamentally changed the nature of human interaction today.

William Gibson, the science fiction author who coined the term "cyberspace" said that no technology is inherently good or evil. It's how we apply it that matters. The same goes for social media. Sharing pictures of good times, promoting your work, and generally staying in touch with friends and family are all obvious pluses. If, however, you're someone who uses social media to "vent" about problems in your life, post cryptic messages that beg for sympathy or attention, publicly complain to companies about customer service, or generally bash things that you don't like—be it a recent episode of *Supergirl* or the president's latest speech—I hope you'll take a moment to pause and realize that your words and thoughts are indeed powerful, and to be careful about what you're bringing to the table and choosing to share with the world.

I am by no means saying that social media can't be used as a platform to critique; the ability to galvanize and mobilize millions around a social protest or other cause for the common good is extraordinarily wonderful. I'm just saying to choose your words carefully; complaining without offering a constructive solution doesn't do much except invite others to wallow with you in misery. Also remember that advocating for what you believe is right doesn't ever have to involve using insulting language. If you can't argue your point without belittling your opponent, then your argument probably isn't very strong.

The rapid advance of technology makes our world smaller every day and connects us in ways that were once unimaginable. Let's respect that ability and decide to always choose our words carefully. Don't ever forget that whoever you're talking to, there's a real person on the other end. Our world can only be as good as what we choose to bring to the table.

We can't stop the advance of technology, but we can commit to using it for good. In that spirit, I ask you to stay mindful and remember that the virtual example you set for your kids is just as important as the real-world one. When you are using social media, use it to spread a little love. Compliment a stranger. Reach out to a loved one you don't see very often. Encourage a young person struggling to establish their career. I think you'll be amazed at what happens as a result.

> Compliment a stranger. Reach out to a loved one you don't see very often. Encourage a young person struggling to establish their career. I think you'll be amazed at what happens as a result.

Layered Chocolate Mousse Cups

481	**8**G	**41**G	**24**G
CALORIES	**PROTEIN**	**FAT**	**CARBS**

SERVES 8

6 oz dark chocolate
(70% cacao)

22 oz heavy cream

1 cup whole milk

1 tbsp salt

6 egg yolks

½ cup sugar

½ cup crumbled brownies
(see brownie recipe
on page 163)

¼ cup dark chocolate
shavings

4 raspberries

½ cup mascarpone

1 Over a water bath, melt chocolate: Place water in a skillet and turn to medium-high heat. Place chopped chocolate in a heat-proof bowl, place the bowl in the water, and stir while the chocolate melts.

2 Bring the cream, milk, and salt to boil and let cool.

3 Whisk yolks and sugar together. Add the cream mixture to the egg yolk mixture using a whisk, making sure not to overmix and scramble eggs.

4 Add egg mixture to chocolate mixture. Mix until smooth.

5 Layer into small cups; a spoonful of mousse followed by crumbled brownies. Repeat until full. Top with chocolate shavings.

6 Garnish with raspberries and marscapone cheese.

Lemon Sponge Cake

229	**5**G	**8**G	**36**G
CALORIES	PROTEIN	FAT	CARBS

SERVES 12

3 cups cake flour

½ tsp salt

2 tsp baking powder

5 tbsp grapeseed oil

¾ cup sugar

3 large eggs

4 lemons, zested

2 oranges, zested

½ cup milk

Confectioner's sugar
 for garnish

1 Preheat an oven to 350 degrees.

2 In a medium bowl, add flour, salt, and baking powder and mix.

3 In large bowl, add grapeseed oil and sugar. Mix together with an electric mixer, incorporating eggs one at a time.

4 Add lemon and orange zest, half the flour, and half the milk and mix together. Once incorporated, mix in remaining milk and flour.

5 In a greased cake pan, add the batter. Bake for approximately 20 minutes.

6 Allow to cool and serve with a dusting of confectioner's sugar.

Cherry-Apple Crisp

288
CALORIES

6G
PROTEIN

10G
FAT

47G
CARBS

SERVES 10

½ lb dried tart cherries

1 cup boiling water

½ lb sweet cherries, pitted

1 lb green apples, peeled, core removed, and sliced

⅓ cup granulated sugar

3 tbsp all-purpose flour

1 tsp vanilla extract

¼ tsp ground cinnamon

4 oz all-purpose flour (about ¾ cup)

1 cup old-fashioned rolled oats

¼ cup packed brown sugar

¼ cup sliced almonds

1 tsp salt

3 oz unsalted butter, melted

1 Combine dried cherries and boiling water in a small bowl; cover and let stand for 30 minutes.

2 Combine dried cherries with soaking liquid, 1 lb sweet cherries, 1 lb apples, sugar, flour, vanilla extract, and cinnamon in a large bowl; stir well.

3 Pour the mixture into a 13x9-inch glass or ceramic baking dish, lightly buttered. Bake at 375 degrees for 40 minutes.

4 In a separate bowl add 4 oz flour, oats, brown sugar, almonds, and salt and stir well. Melt butter in a small bowl, and drizzle over oat mixture and mix well.

5 Remove the fruit from the oven, cover with the streusel topping. Bake for 20 minutes until golden brown. Let stand for 5 minutes serve warm.

CHEF'S TIP   Water can extract sugar from dried fruit, but boiling water does faster. In this case, when the fresh fruit is added to the water, it is quickly infuse with the powerful, tart flavor of the dried cherries, which is quite pronounced in the finished product. You can play with this to suit your own tastes; try replacin the dried cherries with dried apricots, nectarines, peaches, or golden raisins.

Pumpkin Bread Pudding

465	**9**G	**28**G	**45**G
CALORIES	PROTEIN	FAT	CARBS

SERVES 12

2 ½ cups heavy cream

2 ½ cups half and half

4 cloves

1 cinnamon stick

¼ orange, zested

1 tsp ginger powder

1 tsp grated nutmeg

4 egg yolks

4 large eggs

½ cup granulated sugar

½ cup dark brown sugar

1 whole pullman loaf brioche 12-inch loaf (cut into 1-inch cubes)

½ cup dried cherries

½ cup currants

2 oz bourbon

1 In a small sauce pot add heavy cream, half and half, 4 cloves, cinnamon sticks, orange zest, ginger, and nutmeg. Bring to a simmer. Allow ingredients to steep for approximately 1 hour, then strain

2 In a mixing bowl, add egg yolks, eggs, granulated sugar, and dark brown sugar, using a whisk to mix together.

3 Add the infused cream mixture and egg and sugar mixture together.

4 Add cubed pullman loaf to cream and egg mixture. Allow the bread to soak up the batter. Add cherries, currants, and bourbon.

5 In a 10-inch greased cast iron pan, bake in a 350-degree oven for about 45 minutes.

BOREDOM BUILDS CHARACTER— AND CREATIVITY

I get a lot of crap for being against phones at the dinner table. Most of the pushback comes from parents who see no way to break their kids' dependence on YouTube or Angry Birds.

"But Robert, it's the only way to eat a meal with these kids in peace."

"But Robert, all their friends do it."

"But Robert, it's really harmless."

Keeping phones out at the dinner table is detrimental to not only your kids' development, but to your strength as a family unit. Let's address each excuse above.

1 You might buy yourself a few minutes' peace by putting a smartphone in your kids' hands at the dinner table, but the tradeoff is a poor one. The dinner table ought to be the place where kids learn the basic social skills that will serve them as they get older. A child who eats with one hand and scrolls a phone with the other isn't one who's going to be very good at making friends or empathizing with others, to say nothing of being able to hold their own in a business lunch once they've entered the work force. That last point can seem far away when they're young, but it comes up on you incredibly fast. Don't blink—or let it pass by with your kid's head buried in their phone.

2 "But everyone else is doing it" is a sad excuse on many levels. Try looking in the mirror and saying you want your kid to be exactly like everyone else. How does that feel? Terrible? It should.

3 Finally, we reach the fallacy that staying glued to a smartphone throughout one's developmental years is a harmless endeavor. Let me come partway to you on this, and, for the sake of argument, say I'm wrong about excuses 1 and 2. Let's say that kids can learn how to socialize, empathize, and bring conversation to the table without interrupting the endless scroll. Let's say they figure out at a later date how to shine on their own and not be just like everyone else. What major concern still remains? Phone addiction kills boredom, and in turn, creativity. Think about it. When you were a kid and got bored you had to come up with ways to entertain yourself. You made up games to play outside and

when the weather was bad, you created stories with your toys or built a blanket fort and pretended it was a castle. You used your mind. This only happens when you're bored! Logging on every time the unpleasantness of boredom sets in is unnatural and kills this impulse.

Science fiction author Jeff VanderMeer, in his terrific creative writing book, *Wonderbook*, wrote that you can't be a good writer if you're not observing the world around you. I'll take it further. I don't think you can be good at any role that requires cooperation with other people, including all work and personal relationships, if you're always on your phone. Break the habit. You, and everyone around you, deserves better.

S'mores Pie

429	**6**G	**23**G	**51**G
CALORIES	**PROTEIN**	**FAT**	**CARBS**

SERVES 16

4 oz butter

5.3 oz sugar

1 tsp vanilla extract

1 egg

1 cup graham cracker crumbs

1 ⅓ cups flour

1 tsp baking powder

½ tsp salt

20 oz milk chocolate

3 cups miniature marshmallows

4.5 oz bittersweet chocolate

½ cup heavy cream

1 Preheat oven to 350 degrees. Grease a half sheet tray (18x13) or glass Pyrex baking dish.

2 Beat butter, sugar, vanilla, and eggs together, using the paddle attachment on the standup mixer.

3 In a separate bowl, stir together ½ cup graham cracker crumbs, flour, baking powder, and salt. Combine with sugar/vanilla /egg mixture.

4 Press half the dough into already greased half sheet pan and bake for 15 minutes.

5 Melt the milk chocolate in a saucepan or in a microwave. Pour into freshly baked graham cracker pie shell. Top with marshmallows.

6 Scatter ½ cup of graham cracker crumbs on top of the bars and bake for an additional 10 minutes.

7 Make chocolate ganache: In a separate small pot add heavy cream and bring to a boil, slowly incorporate bittersweet chocolate using a whisk. Once all chocolate is incorporated, keep warm being careful not to burn.

8 Finish the pie by blow torching the marshmallows or briefly placing the pie under the broiler and watching carefully. Top with hot chocolate ganache.

Brown Betty

229	3G	7G	41G
CALORIES	**PROTEIN**	**FAT**	**CARBS**

SERVES 6

5 large Granny Smith
  apples, cubed

1 cup apple cider

3 tbsp brown sugar

2 tbsp butter

3 slices whole wheat bread,
  cut into 1-inch cubes

3 tbsp chopped walnuts

1 Preheat oven to 350 degrees.

2 Combine apples, apple cider, and 1 tbsp brown sugar in a sauce pan. Cook over medium heat for approximately 8 minutes.

3 Grease a glass Pyrex baking dish with 1 tbsp butter and spread apples across the bottom.

4 Melt the rest of the butter and toss sugar, whole wheat bread, and walnuts.

5 Cover apples with the bread and walnut topping.

6 Bake for 15 minutes. Let cool and serve.

GET THE KIDS INVOLVED   Cubing bread is a safe way to teach a kid some basic knife skills since they don't need a sharp knife; they can just use a regular table knife. Just have them slice the bread one piece at a time to avoid ripping and tearing.

Warm Fruit with Mascarpone

348 CALORIES	**4G** PROTEIN	**26G** FAT	**28G** CARBS

SERVES 4

½ cup fresh cherries, seeds removed and halved

½ cup blackberries

½ cup strawberries

4 tbsp mild honey

4 large basil leaves, torn

½ cup blueberries

½ cup raspberries

8 vanilla beans, halved lengthwise

8 oz mascarpone

6 small basil sprigs

1 Combine cherries, blackberries, half of the strawberries, and honey in a small saucepan over low heat; cook 8 minutes or until slightly warmed, gently stirring occasionally. Remove from heat; stir in basil.

2 In a separate bowl mix the blueberries, raspberries, and the remaining strawberries. Set aside.

3 Scrape seeds from vanilla bean. Combine seeds and mascarpone in a small bowl, stirring well.

4 Spoon about ¼ cup cheese mixture into 4 small bowls. Top each serving with about ¼ cup warm fruit mixture. Top each serving with ¼ cup remaining fresh berries and a basil sprig.

CHEF'S TIP It's so easy to make a delicious dessert with warm fruit that it almost feels like cheating. Don't believe me? Try old-fashioned baked apples. Ju. core a few apples, slice them in half, dust them with cinammon and nutmeg, an place them on a baking sheet in a 375-degree oven for 30 minutes. It tastes a lot like apple pie filling, but with way fewer calories—and it's totally effortless.

Peanut Butter & Jelly Pie

550 CALORIES	**15**G PROTEIN	**38**G FAT	**29**G CARBS

SERVES 16

FOR THE CRUST

2 cups flour

1 tbsp sugar

½ lb butter, cubed

½ cup very cold shortening

½ cup ice water

FOR THE FILLING

3 cups peanut butter

2 cups cream cheese

½ cup confectionary sugar

½ cup grape jam

THE CRUST

1 Combine flour, salt, and sugar into a food processor with the blade attachment.

2 Pulse butter and shortening into the flour mixture. Incorporate ice cold water to the mixture.

3 Wrap in plastic wrap and place in refrigerator for an hour.

4 Using a rolling pin and a liberal amount of flour, roll dough into a circle that fits into your pie pan. Place dough in pan and poke small holes in the dough.

5 Place a piece of parchment paper in the center of pie crust, weigh down dough with dried beans.

6 Bake crust at 375 degrees for approximately 20 minutes.

7 Remove pie dough from the oven and lift out weight. Using a fork, poke small holes in the pie dough to avoid bubbling.

8 Place dough back into oven and cook for another 20 minutes and chill.

THE FILLING

1 In a stand mixer, whip peanut butter and cream cheese, and mix on medium for approximately 2 minutes.

2 Add confectionary sugar to the mixture and lower the speed until incorporated.

3 Take filling and place in chilled baked pie dough.

4 Refrigerate for 2 or more hours, then cut pie into eight equal slices. Spoon a small amount of grape jam on each slice and serve with ice cold milk.

MAKE YOUR KITCHEN
THE ULTIMATE
CLASSROOM

Forging better relationships, creating lasting memories, nourishing souls as you feed bodies... there are a lot of emotional reasons to bring your kids into the kitchen. Then there are the health reasons: One study showed that when we eat out, we consume an additional 200 calories per day. If you eat out every day, that's 1,400 calories per week, 5,600 per month, or 67,200 per year, which—when you consider the fact that you need to burn 3,500 calories to burn one pound of fat—adds up to almost 20 pounds gained in a year. World-class restaurants and fast food eateries alike take shortcuts to your taste buds with lots of extra fat, salt, and sugar. It's no wonder we find ourselves in the midst of a dire health crisis where nearly a third of the population is obese. So first and foremost, teaching your kids to cook gives them the tools they need to avoid the trap of eating out constantly, which will make them much healthier in the long run.

There is a third reason to cook with your kids. The kitchen is the ultimate classroom, a place where math, biology, chemistry, and history all come into play. Let me explain.

MATH: Addition and subtraction are components of basic measuring, and fractions are unavoidable in recipe writing. In the kitchen, kids learn these in a memorable way, not just as numbers on paper.

BIOLOGY: Eggs are a great lesson in and of themselves; just make sure you explain that the eggs in your fridge are never fertilized and that you're not eating an unborn chicken. Likewise, every piece of meat offers an anatomy lesson. Never mind kids, a lot of adults aren't aware that meat is muscle. If you're shaky on where various cuts of meat come from—or with any of these lessons—look up the answers before passing on bad info.

CHEMISTRY: Chefs have the power to transform food and create something new,

and heat is the element that allows a chef do just that. Once you apply heat, cell structures begin to break down and when you start adding other ingredients to the mix, the magic of chemistry—or transformation—begins. Every piece of food, from caramelized onions to fried eggs, from boiled noodles to bran muffins, offers a unique window into this incredible process.

HISTORY: Sandwiches take their name from the Earl of Sandwich, who was a habitual gambler and liked serving meat between two slices of bread so he could easily eat at the card table. One of my all-time favorite snacks—buffalo wings—were created at the Anchor Bar in Buffalo, NY, by a chef with very little in the pantry but with creativity to spare. Every food has a story to tell. Do a little bit of research before you get started and you can turn every meal into a learning experience.

Remember: Having your kids with you in the kitchen is like having your own interactive cooking show. You don't have to stick with just these topics or do a tremendous amount of research; you could simply teach your kids about your personal connection to the dish. Just make them a part of everything and narrate what you're doing. Even something as mundane as cleaning out the fridge can be brought to life. Show them how you can tell when food is spoiled, or that when greens start to turn yellow or soggy that they're losing their flavor and nutrients.

Give your kids credit. Some of this might go over their head in the short-term, but they will catch up! Some gold fish will grow to the size of the bowl, so give them a big bowl to swim in.

ACKNOWLEDGEMENTS

I would like to extend a heartfelt thank you to my culinary team for all their hard work on this book. Special thanks go to my Corporate Chef Brian Goodman and VP of Concept Development Shane Cash, whose long hours planning, prepping, and grinding away in a hot kitchen helped make it possible and to my VP of Culinary Affairs Darryl Moiles for his expertise and support.

Additional thanks go to all of Team Irvine, especially my co-author and GM of *Robert Irvine Magazine*, Matt Tuthill for helping me put my thoughts to paper, VP of Finance and Marketing Joshua Lingenfelter for his business expertise, Personal Assistant Ryan Coyne for his logistical know-how, and my Chief Operating Officer Justin Leonard for always keeping the big picture in focus on all my projects.

I'd like to also extend a very big thank you to Ian Spanier for another wonderful photo shoot and making me—and all my food—look great, to Sean Otto for the beautiful design work and layout of this book, and to my editor Adam Bible for his steady hand throughout the process.

We can only be as good as the people we surround ourselves with. As I look around at the people in my personal and business relationships, I recognize that I've been extraordinarily blessed in life.

ABOUT ROBERT IRVINE

With three decades of culinary experience accrued around the world, award-winning Chef Robert Irvine is best known for hosting some of the Food Network's highest rated shows including *Restaurant: Impossible* and *Dinner: Impossible*. He is the owner of two restaurants: Robert Irvine's Public House at the Tropicana Las Vegas and Fresh Kitchen By Robert Irvine, located inside the Pentagon. He is the author of three previous cookbooks: *Mission: Cook!*, *Impossible to Easy*, and *Fit Fuel*. A tireless advocate for the military, he is the founder of The Robert Irvine Foundation (RobertIrvine Foundation.org), which supports veterans and various military causes. Get tickets to his live show, *Robert Irvine LIVE* at chefirvine.com/ri-live. Download back issues of his digital publication, *Robert Irvine Magazine*, for free at RobertIrvineMagazine.com.